Karen's LOL, OMG And Knock Knock Jokes Collection

The 4 Books Compilation Set For Kids

Karen J. Bun

This book consists of:
1. Karen's OMG Joke Books For Kids - Funny, Silly, Dumb Jokes that Will Make Children Roll on the Floor Laughing
2. Karen's Dad Jokes - The Bad, Funny, Clean And LOL Jokes For The Cool Dad
3. Karen's Knock Knock Jokes For Kids - The Unbreakable Door That No One Ever Got Past
4. Karen's Unicorn Knock Knock Jokes - The Magical Door That Spurts Rainbow Endlessly

Karen's OMG Joke Book for Kids

Funny, Silly, Dumb Jokes that Will Make Children Roll on the Floor Laughing

Karen J. Bun

Table of Contents

Bluesource And Friends

Introduction

Chapter 1 Kids' Riddles

Chapter 2: Kids' Knock-Knock Jokes

Chapter 3: Kids' Silly, Dumb Jokes

Chapter 4: Longer Dumb Jokes

Chapter 5: Kids' Puns and Other Jokes

Chapter 6: Quirky Questions

Chapter 7: Books Never Written

Conclusion

Bluesource And Friends

This book is brought to you by Bluesource And Friends, a happy book publishing company.

Our motto is **"Happiness Within Pages."**

We promise to deliver amazing value to readers with our books. We also appreciate honest book reviews from our readers.

Connect with us on our Facebook page www.facebook.com/bluesourceandfriends and stay tuned to our latest book promotions and free giveaways.

Don't forget to claim your FREE book

https://tinyurl.com/karenbrainteasers

Also check out our best seller book

https://tinyurl.com/lateralthinkingpuzzles

Introduction

Congratulations on downloading the book *Karen's OMG Joke Book for Kids: Funny, Silly, Dumb Jokes that Will Make Children Roll on the Floor Laughing*. I thank you for downloading it. The following chapters will make your child howl with laughter. The first chapter is filled with riddles that will make their sides hurt. This book has everything from the classic knock-knock jokes to bad puns that will make even you shake your head! There are also a few surprises along the way! Your child will read some 'quirky questions' as well as 'books never written.' This book was designed for kids between the ages of seven and twelve. They will experience short, sweet, and simple jokes as well as longer jokes that grab their attention and deliver a forceful one-liner!

There are plenty of books like this on the market, so thanks again for choosing this one! Every effort was made to ensure your child will enjoy what they are about to read. Please enjoy!

Chapter 1 Kids' Riddles

Q: My outside can be thrown and my inside can be cooked. My outside can be eaten and my inside can be thrown. What am I?

A: A corn's cob. The stalk is thrown and the corn is cooked. The inside can be thrown once the corn has been eaten.

Q: I have three hands but I cannot use them to clap. What am I?
A: I'm a clock.

Q: You can only use me once you have broken me. What am I?
A: I'm an egg.

Q: I can't see even though I still have an eye. What do you think I am?
A: A needle

Q: The most water can only be held by what letter?
A: The 'C'

Q: There was a blue, one-story house. The couch was blue. The rugs were blue. Even the cat was blue. What color do you think the stairs were?

A: The house didn't have any stairs. It was only one-story.

Q: All through winter, I have lived. Once I die during summer, roots start to grow from the top. What am I?
A: An ice cycle

Q: Even the world's strongest person can't hold this for more than sixty seconds although it is as light as a feather. What is it?
A: They can't hold their breath.

Q: A cowboy rode into town on Wednesday. He stayed for three days and left the same town on Wednesday. How can this be possible?
A: The cowboy's horse's name is Wednesday.

Q: How is it possible for a person to go without sleep for 8 days straight?
A: They only sleep at night.

Q: Moneyless people have this and it is needed by wealthy people. You will eventually die once you've eaten it. What is it?
A: It's nothing.

Q: Which has more weight, a pound of cement or a pound of paper?
A: Both of them weigh a pound, so they are equal.

Q: What is used more by other people but is always yours?
A: Your name

Q: I can't open doors even though I'm full of keys. What am I?
A: I'm a piano.

Q: I have four fingers and one thumb, but I am not a living thing. What am I?
A: A glove

Q: How many months in the year have twenty-eight days in them?
A: All of the months have twenty-eight days!

Q: Which invention helps you to see through walls?
A: A window

Q: What occurs one time in a minute, two times in a moment, and never in 100 years?
A: 'M'

Q: As it dries, it gets wetter?
A: A towel gets wetter as it dries.

Q: Everyone has one of these, and it is impossible to lose. What is it?

A: A shadow

Q: How much distance can be run by a fox into the woods?
A: Only halfway. Otherwise, it would be running out of the woods.

Q: Take away a single letter, I become even. At first, I'm very odd. What am I?
A: Seven

Q: This will never fall back down but will always go up.
A: Your age

Q: What word has a T and starts and ends with a T?
A: It's a teapot.

Q: I get shorter as I get old, although when I was young, I am tall. What am I?
A: A candle

Q: What word is spelled wrong in every single dictionary?
A: Wrong

Q: I start with the letter 'E', and I only have one letter in me. What am I?
A: I'm an envelope.

Q: How does a leopard change its spots?
A: It gets up and moves to a different one.

Q: What is really hard to get out of but super easy to get into?
A: Trouble

Q: If a mom, a dad, and their son were not underneath an umbrella, how did they not get wet?
A: It wasn't raining.

Q: Troy's parents had three sons. They were named Snap, Crackle, and what?
A: Troy

Q: You bought me for dinner, but you have never eaten me. What am I?
A: A fork and knife

Q: After a train crashed, every single person died. Who survived?
A: All of the couples

Q: I still can't see even though I have four eyes.
A: Mississippi

Q: Even though I'm staying in the same spot, I can still travel all around the world. What do you think am I?
A: A stamp

Q: The English alphabet contains how many letters?
A: There are eighteen. 3 in 'the', 7 in 'English', and 8 in 'alphabet'.

Q: I can still hold liquid even though I have holes. What am I?
A: A sponge

Q: What can you never answer yes to?
A: Are you asleep?

Q: When everything seems to be going wrong, what can you always count on?
A: Your fingers can always be counted.

Q: What's always ahead of you but you can never see?
A: The future

Q: Where can you find, cities, towns, countries, and shops but no people?
A: A map

Q: Bob walked for half an hour in the rain and didn't get a hair on his head wet. He didn't have an umbrella or a hat. How did he do it?
A: He is bald.

Q: I cannot hear even though I have ears. What am I?
A: Corn

Q: There are no doors or windows in this kind of room. What room is this?
A: A mushroom

Q: What do you take in when it isn't being used, but throw out when you need to use it?
A: An anchor

Q: I have difficulty standing up by myself even though I have thousands of legs. I don't have a head even if my neck is long. What am I?
A: I'm a broom.

Q: I can't walk although I have legs.
A: A table

Q: What never moves but always goes up?
A: Stairs

Q: Which side does an egg fall when it was laid by a rooster at the top of a barn?
A: A rooster can't lay eggs. Hens do.

Q: When is a door not a door?
A: When it's ajar

Q: You can't hold me. You can only catch me. What am I?
A: A cold

Q: What can be deadly and quick while it gathers by the beach?
A: Sand

Q: Be careful! You are at a railroad crossing. Be sure that there are no cars. Can you spell this without any 'r's'?
A: T-H-I-S

Q: I have no door, but I hold keys. I have no place to stay even though I have some space. You aren't allowed to leave even if you can enter me. What am I?
A: I'm a keyboard.

Q: I can run and drop but can't walk. What am I?
A: A drop of water

Q: If there are five apples and you take two, how many do you have?
A: You have two.

Q: I have wings, and I can fly. I am not a bird, so what am I?
A: An airplane

Q: What is always late and never present?
A: Later

Q: I can be big, white, dirty, or wicked. What am I?
A: A lie

Q: What do cats, dogs, fish, and turtles all have in common?
A: The letter 'S'

Q: Almost everybody needs me, asks for me, gives me but hardly anyone takes me. What am I?
A: Advice

Q: What am I that can point in every direction, but I can't get anywhere by myself?
A: Your finger

Q: I am not your clothes, but I cover your body. What am I that get thinner the more that I am used?
A: A bar of soap

Q: What am I that never break even if I fall?
A: Nightfall

Q: I'm known as the first of all of my kind. I am never found in trucks and never on buses. I'm not used in Ohio, but I am used in Arkansas.
A: The letter 'A'

Q: I have two backbones and thousands upon thousands of ribs.
A: A railroad

Q: I will always point you in the right direction. You must follow my lead or you will get astray. What am I that will never say more than two words at a time?
A: The signage of 'one way'

Q: I can run constantly without getting tired. I frustrate people without having to move. What am I?
A: A runny nose

Q: What am I that the more of me you leave behind, the more of me you take.
A: I'm footsteps.

Q: I'm heavy forward, but backward I am not. What am I?
A: I'm a ton.

Q: What am I that get bigger the more you've taken from me?
A: I'm a hole.

Q: What am I that if I'm with you, you will want to tell me. But once you tell me, I am no longer with you.
A: I'm a secret.

Q: Everyone has a view of me but doesn't pay attention. Without one, though, everyone would look crazy. What am I?
A: I'm a nose.

Q: It will be harder for you to grab me the more you move with me.
A: Your breath

Q: Do what he says, and you will be okay. Don't and you will lose the game. Who is he?
A: Simon

Q: Bugs don't like this vegetable. It may be the only one they don't move toward. What is it?
A: It's a squash.

Q: You can see me in the water sometimes, but I am always dry.
A: A reflection

Q: I only repeat the last word you say. The more I repeat, the softer I get. I can't be seen but I can be heard. What am I?
A: An echo

Q: Take me for a spin, and I will make you cool. If you use me in the winter, you are a fool. What am I?
A: A fan

Q: You can't really see me, but you can touch me. You can't throw me away but you can throw me out.
A: Your back

Q: What am I that will halt on green and continue on red when you are dealing with me?
A: I'm a watermelon.

Q: Shadows follow me wherever I go. I have no eyes but I can produce tears. I have no wings but I can glide above you. What am I?

A: I'm a cloud.

Q: He says I love you when I told him. He smiles back at me when I smile at him and looks back at me when I look at him. Who is he?
A: His reflection

Q: I go around all cities, towns, and villages but I never go inside anywhere.
A: A road

Q: What do you think I am that can die when I have no life?
A: A battery

Q: When you wave my flag, I took and give away the one you receive?
A: I'm a mailbox.

Q: I'm a five-letter word and very big and hard. I am alone when two letters are removed from me.
A: Stone

Q: I know a word that has six letters. Take away just one letter, twelve is what remains. What word am I?
A: Dozens

Q: Wash me and then I'm not clean. Don't wash me and I am.
A: Water

Q: I live without needing to breathe but I'm always cold. I am never dehydrated but I am hardly ever drinking. What am I?
A: I'm a fish.

Q: At the same time, I go down and up. I am present-tense and past-tense, too. What am I?
A: See-saw

Q: I always run, but there is no way I can walk. I sometimes make small noises but I am not talking. I also have a bed, but I never use it. I never eat but I have a mouth. What am I?
A: A river

Q: When I am changing my jacket, loud noises will be made. I begin to weigh less the more I become larger. What am I?
A: Popcorn

Q: What am I that becomes dirty when I'm white.
A: A blackboard

Q: I shave 30 times a day, but I still have hair.
A: A barber

Q: I do not have a head, but I have a long straight neck. What am I?
A: A bottle

Q: I stay where I am when I go off. What am I?
A: An alarm clock

Q: I do not ask questions but I need an answer.
A: A telephone

Q: What am I that go up and down all of the time, but I never move?
A: The temperature

Q: What do you think I am when I am weightless and as large as an elephant? What am I?
A: I'm an elephant's shadow.

Q: It is not wanted by the person who carved it. It's not needed yet by the person who bought it. It was never seen by the person who used it. What is this thing?
A: A coffin

Q: What do you call a thing that has a head and a foot but has 4 legs?
A: A bed

Q: You can never eat me for lunch or dinner. What am I?
A: Breakfast

Q: What do you call me when you can hold me without touching me?
A: A conversation

Q: I don't need to eat but I have teeth. What do you call me?
A: A comb

Q: What do you call something that can be made but cannot be seen?
A: Noise

Q: Orange is my color and I sound like a parrot. What am I?
A: Carrot

Q: I have flies and four wheels. What do you call me?
A: A garbage pick-up truck

Q: Which part of the turkey has the most feathers?
A: The outside

Chapter 2: Kids' Knock-Knock Jokes

Knock, knock

Who's there?

Figs.

Figs who?

Figs the doorbell, it's not working right!

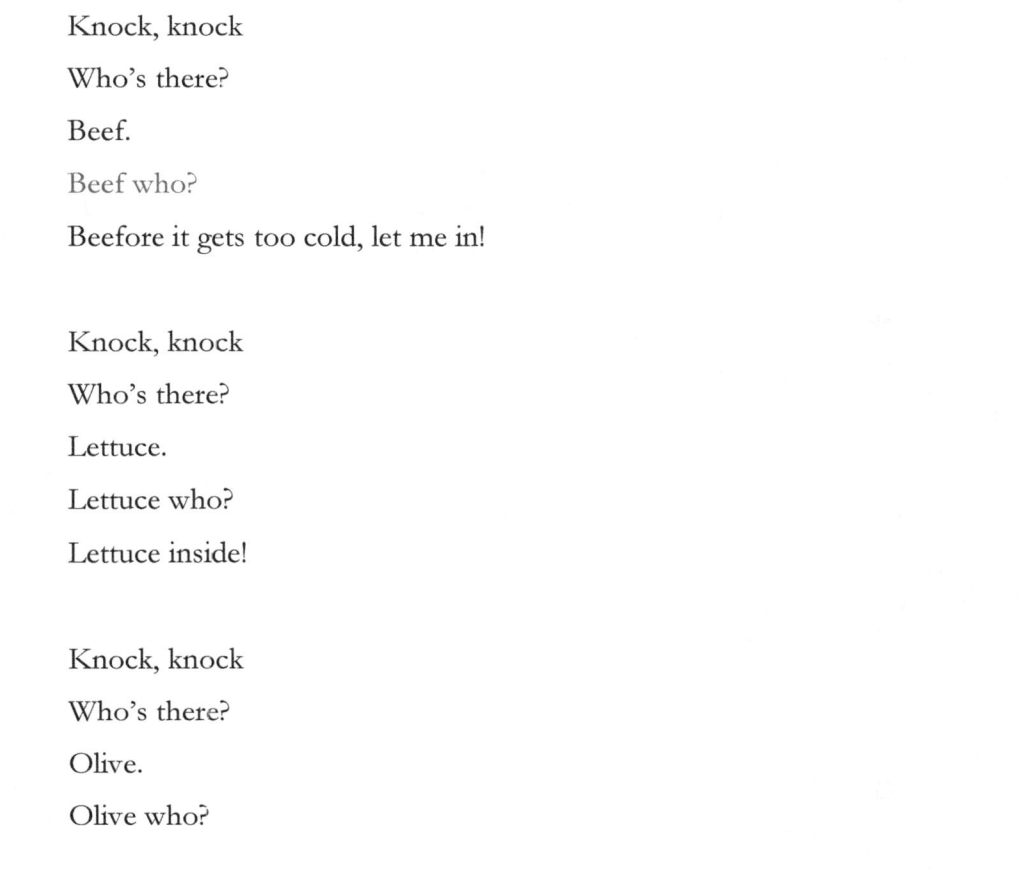

Knock, knock

Who's there?

Beef.

Beef who?

Beefore it gets too cold, let me in!

Knock, knock

Who's there?

Lettuce.

Lettuce who?

Lettuce inside!

Knock, knock

Who's there?

Olive.

Olive who?

Olive next door?

Knock, knock
Who's there?
Ice cream.
Ice cream who?
Ice cream for ice cream!

Knock, knock
Who's there?
Turnip.
Turnip who?
Turnip the volume, I can't hear anything!

Knock, knock
Who's there?
Orange.
Orange who?
Orange you working on your project?

Knock, knock

Who's there?
Mustache
Mustache who?

I mustache you something but I'll shave it for later if you won't open the door for me!

Who's there?
Annie.
Annie who?
You don't believe Annie thing I say!

   Knock, knock
   Who's there?
   Voodoo.
   Voodoo who?
   Voodoo you want to go with on your prom?

   Knock, knock
   Who's there?
   Candice.
   Candice who?
   Candice be the right thing to say?

   Knock, knock
   Who's there?
   Donut.
   Donut who?
   Donut ask anyone around here.

Knock, knock
Who's there?
Ada.
Ada who?
Ada spaghetti on my meal.

Knock, knock
Who's there?
Anita.
Anita who?
Anita buy shoes, please?

Knock, knock
Who's there?
Annie.
Annie who?
Annie body going to let me in?

Knock, knock
Who's there?
Ben.
Ben who?
Ben singing that song three times. Cut it out already!

Knock, knock
Who's there?
Frank.
Frank who?
I want to Frank you for making me smile.

Knock, knock
Who's there?
Doris.
Doris who?
Doris open, come in.

Knock, knock
Who's there?
Howard.
Howard who?
Howard you guess what that is?

Knock, knock
Who's there?
Isabell.
Isabell who?
Isabell ringing? Somebody might be outside.

Knock, knock

Who's there?

Justin.

Justin who?

Justin town. I have to check on some things.

Knock, knock

Who's there?

Ken

Ken who?

Ken I have more soup, please?

Knock, knock

Who's there?

Lena.

Lena who?

Lena bit closer and you'll know who.

Knock, knock

Who's there?

Nana.

Nana who?

Nana my things are missing.

Knock, knock

Who's there?

Nobel,

Nobel who?

Nobel. That's why I have been knocking for quite some time now.

Knock, knock

Who's there?

Windy.

Windy who?

Windy dog ran, it bumped on my knee.

Knock, knock

Who's there?

Will.

Will who?

Will I meet the man of my dreams someday?

Knock, knock

Who's there?

Cow go.

Cow go who?

No, cow go moo! A cow never said who.

Knock, knock

Who's there?

Goat.

Goat who?

Goat to the pharmacy and buy me some medicine, please.

Knock, knock
Who's there?
Some bunny.
Some bunny who?
Some bunny has finally won the jackpot prize!

Knock, knock
Who's there?
Amarillo.
Amarillo who?
Amarillo kind friend.

Knock, knock
Who's there?
Amish.
Amish who?
Amish our old days.

Knock, knock
Who's there?
Avenue.
Avenue who?

Avenue done makeup before?

Knock, knock
Who's there?
Cash.
Cash who?
I prefer eating peanuts than cash who.

Knock, knock
Who's there?
Dishes.
Dishes who?
Dishes a great place you've got.

Knock, knock
Who's there?
Doctor.
Doctor who?
That is such a great show!

Knock, knock
Who's there?
I'm too short to reach the doorbell.
I'm too short to reach the doorbell who?
No, really. I'm too short.

Knock, knock
Who's there?
Dozen.
Dozen who?
Dozen one know who holds the keys?

Knock, knock
Who's there?
Leaf.
Leaf who?
Leaf him alone. He's wounded.

Knock, knock
Who's there?
Howl.
Howl who?
Howl you remember me when I'm gone?

Knock, knock
Who's there?
Needle.
Needle who?
Do you needle bit help on your homework?

Knock, knock
Who's there?
Police.
Police who?
Police, may I have some cash?

Knock, knock
Who's there?
Radio.
Radio who?
I'm coming up, either you're radio or not.

Knock, knock
Who's there?
Water.
Water who?
Water you doing out there?

Knock, knock
Who's there?
Tank.
Tank who?
Tank you for welcoming me here.

Knock, knock

Who's there?

Witches.

Witches who?

Witches the simplest method to use?

Knock, knock

Who's there?

Wooden shoe.

Wooden shoe who?

Wooden shoe be happier if she's here?

Knock, knock

Who's there?

Harry.

Harry who?

Harry now or else I'll leave you behind.

Knock, knock

Who's there?

Canoe.

Canoe who?

Canoe please help me carry these things?

Knock, knock

Who's there?

I am.

I am who?

How do you not know who you are!

Knock, knock

Who's there?

Yah.

Yah who?

Google is what I prefer.

Knock, knock

Who's there?

Alpaca.

Alpaca who?

Alpaca first aid kit for our trip tomorrow just to be sure.

Knock, knock

Who's there?

See, you forgot me already!

Knock, knock

Who's there?

Owl says.

Owl says who?

Yes, they do.

Knock, knock
Who's there?
Kanga
Kanga who?
It's not kanga who, it's a kangaroo.

Knock, knock
Who's there?
Beats
Beats who?
Beats me.

Knock, knock
Who's there?
Deja.
Deja who?
Knock, knock

Knock, knock
Who's there?
A broken pencil.
A broken pencil who?
It's pointless, so don't worry about it.

Knock, knock
Who's there?
Europe.
Europe who?
No, I'm not a poo! You're the poo!

Knock, knock
Who's there?
Theodore.
Theodore who?
Theodore was open that's why the thief entered easily.

Knock, knock
Who's there?
Etchy.
Etchy who?
Bless you!

Knock, knock
Who's there?
Spell.
Spell who?
W-H-O.

Knock, knock

Who's there?

Mikey.

Mikey who?

I left Mikey on the car.

Knock, knock

Who's there?

Herd.

Herd who?

I herd you call my name. Why?

Knock, knock

Who's there?

Venice.

Venice who?

Venice she going to school?

Knock, knock

Who's there?

Iran.

Iran who?

Iran straight from the grocery store.

Knock, knock

Who's there?

Adore.

Adore who?

Adore is open last night.

Knock, knock

Who's there?

Orange.

Orange who?

Orange you going to say you love me before you leave?

Chapter 3: Kids' Silly, Dumb Jokes

Q: A sleeping dinosaur is called what?
A: A dino-snore!

Q: What is fast but loud and crunchy at the same time?
A: A rocket-chip!

Q: Why did the teddy bear pass on dessert?
A: He was stuffed!

Q: What has thousands of ears, but it cannot hear?
A: A cornfield!

Q: What did the left eye say to the right eye?
A: There's something between us and it smells!

Q: What do you get when you come across a vampire and a snowman?
A: Frost-bite!

Q: What was said to the fork by the plate?
A: Dinner is on me!

Q: What is the reason behind the small boy eating his homework?
A: He heard from his teacher that it was a piece of cake!

Q: When you are looking for something, why is it always in the last place you look?
A: Because when you find it, you stop looking for it!

Q: Two pickles fell out of a jar and onto the counter. What did one say to the other?
A: Dill with it.

Q: After eating their supper, how did the Dalmatians react?
A: That hit the spot!

Q: Why did the group of kids cross the park?
A: They needed to get to the other slide!

Q: How does a vampire start writing a letter?
A: Tomb it may concern!

Q: What do you call a droid that takes a different route?
A: R2 detour

Q: How do you stop the astronaut baby from crying?
A: You rocket back and forth!

Q: What was the witches' favorite subject in middle school?
A: Spelling!

Q: How do you make a lemon drop?
A: You let the lemon fall!

Q: What do you call a duck that gets 100% on all of its school projects?
A: A wise quacker!

Q: What kind of water cannot freeze?
A: Hot water!

Q: What sort of tree fits in your hand?
A: A palm tree!

Q: Why did the cracker go to the hospital?
A: Because he felt really crummy!

Q: Why did the baby strawberry start crying?
A: Because its mom and dad were in a jam!

Q: What was the question being asked to the mommy corn by the baby corn?
A: Where is popcorn?

Q: What is worse than raining cats and dogs?
A: Hailing taxis!

Q: Where would you find a penguin?
A: Wherever you lost him!

Q: Which animal is always at a baseball game?
A: A bat!

Q: What always falls in winter but never gets hurt?
A: Snow!

Q: What do you call a ghost's true love?
A: His ghoulfriend!

Q: What building in Los Angeles has the most stories?
A: The public library!

Q: How do you know the ocean is friendly or not?
A: See if it waves!

Q: What is a tornado's favorite game to play at parties?
A: Twister!

Q: How does the moon cut his hair?

A: Eclipse it!

Q: How do you get a squirrel to like you?
A: You gotta act like a nutcase!

Q: What do you call two birds in love?
A: Tweethearts!

Q: How does a scientist freshen his breath?
A: He experi-mints!

Q: How are false teeth like stars?
A: They come out at night!

Q: How can you tell a vampire is getting sick?
A: He starts coffin!

Q: Finding that in your apple, there's a complete worm is less bad than what?
A: Finding a worm cut in half! That means you already ate half!

Q: What is a computer's favorite snack?
A: Computer chips!

Q: What did the cow hear from the apple?

A: Nothing. Apples cannot speak!

Q: When does a cucumber become a pickle?
A: Whenever it goes through a jarring experience!

Q: What do you think of that new diner on the mood?
A: The food was okay, but the atmosphere was awful!

Q: What is the reason why a balloon cannot be given to Elsa?
A: The reason is that it will be let go by her!

Q: How do you make the octopus laugh?
A: With ten-tickles!

Q: What did the finger hear from the nose?
A: Don't pick on me anymore!

Q: Why did the little girl bring a ladder to school?
A: Because she wanted to go to high school!

Q: What is a vampire's favorite fruit?
A: A blood orange!

Q: What do elves learn in English class?
A: The elf-abet!

Q: Why can't the karaoke be sung by the pony?
A: Because his voice was a little hoarse!

Q: Why are school dances being avoided by the skeleton?
A: Because he had no body to dance with!

Q: What do you call a pair of bananas?
A: Slippers

Q: Why is the doctor visited by the banana?
A: Because the banana doesn't peel well.

Q: A fake noodle is called what?
A: An impasta!

Q: How do you fix a cracked pumpkin?
A: You use a pumpkin patch!

Q: What sort of award did the dentist receive?
A: A little plaque!

Q: A sticky hair is a characteristic of bees because?
A: A honeycomb is what they use!

Q: An example of bad liars is the ghost. What is the reason for this?
  A: Because they are transparent!

Q: How was the small flower greeted by the big flower?
A: Hey, bud!

Q: What did the astronaut say when he crashed into the planet?
A: I Apollo-gize!

Q: Why did the orange lose the race?
A: He ran out of juice!

Q: Which dinosaur has the best vocabulary?
A: The thesaurus!

Q: What did one strand of DNA say to her boyfriend strand of DNA?
A: Do these genes make my butt look big?

Q: Why didn't the dogs want to dance at the ball?
A: They have two left feet!

Q: What was being said to the toilet friend from a healthy toilet?
A: You seem a bit flushed!

Q: What is the reason the woman put her money in the freezer?
A: She wanted some cold hard cash!

Q: Why couldn't the astronaut book a room on the moon?
A: Because the moon was full!

Q: What do you call a snowman that is getting old?
A: Water!

Q: Why did the superhero flush his toilet?
A: Because it was his doody!

Q: Where do cows go for entertainment?
A: The mooo-vies!

Q: What does a spider's bride wear?
A: A webbing dress!

Q: What is the smartest creature on earth?
A: A spelling bee

Q: How did the preschoolers learn how to make banana splits?
A: They went to sundae school!

Q: What is the absolute worst thing about throwing a party in space?

A: You have to plan it!

Q: Why did the policeman go to the baseball game?
A: Because he overheard someone had stolen a base so he went to check it out!

Q: Two pairs of pant are worn by golfers at the tournament. What is the reason for this?
A: It was in case they got a hole in one!

Q: What sort of shoes do robbers wear?
A: Sneak-ers!

Q: What do you call two guys hanging out on a curtain?
A: Curt and Rod

Q: Why was the Math book so sad?
A: It was dealing with too many problems!

Q: What time would it be when Godzilla came to hang out?
A: Time to run!

Q: Why did the dog do so well in school?
A: Because he was the teacher's pet!

Q: Why did the egg get thrown out of class?
A: Because he wouldn't stop telling yolks!

Q: What did one penny say to the other while having a conversation?
A: We make perfect cents!

Q: What is the reason behind arresting the belt?
A: Because some pants were being held up by it!

Q: Why did the computer go to the hospital?
A: It became sick with a virus!

Q: Where does the president keep his armies?
A: In his sleeves!

Q: What remark did one firefly receive from the other?
A: You're glowing, girl!

Q: Why did the cucumber blush?
A: He saw the salad dressing!

Q: What do you call a blind dinosaur?
A: Do-you-think-he-saw-us!

Q: How do you catch an entire school of fish?

A: With bookworms!

Q: Why did the mushroom like to party so much?
A: Because he was fungi!

Q: What do you call a guy lying on the front porch?
A: Matt

Q: What do snowmen call their annual ball?
A: The snowball!

Q: If you've seen a spaceman, what will you do?
A: I will be parking my car.

Q: What do cows read?
A: Cattle-logs

Q: Where do young cows eat lunch?
A: In the calf-ateria!

Q: What did the policeman say to his stomach?
A: Stop! You are under a vest!

Q: What do birds give out in their Christmas stockings?
A: Tweets!

Q: How do mountains stay warm in the winter?
A: Snowcaps!

Q: How did the calendar become well-liked?
A: Because he went on so many dates!

Q: What is the reason why the broom is not always on time?
A: It over swept!

Q: Near the sea is where seagulls prefer to live. What is the reason behind this?
A: They will be bagels if they will live by the bay?

Q: After tripping and falling over, what did the horse exclaimed?
A: I fell and can't giddy up!

Q: The girl volcano heard this from the boy volcano. What is it?
A: I lava you!

Q: Name the kind of car that is driven by the girlfriend of Mickey Mouse.
A: A Minnie-van

Q: When you see a sick bird, what will you give it?

A: A special tweetment!

Q: Fishes are wise. Why is that?
A: Because they are always in schools!

Q: What animal has more lives than a cat?
A: A frog. They croak every night!

Q: What musical instrument is always in the bathroom next to the sink?
A: A tuba toothpaste!

Q: Where do pencils take vacations?
A: Pencil-vania!

Q: What kind of music do rabbits and frogs like the best?
A: Hip-hop!

Q: Eight heard this from zero. What is it?
A: Nice belt!

Q: The neck scarf heard this from the snowcap. What is it?
A: Hey, neck scarf, hang around. I will go up ahead.

Q: What time of day do ducks wake up?

A: They wake up at the quack of dawn!

Q: What does the lion say when he first meets another animal in the jungle?
A: Hi, I'm a lion. Pleased to eat you!

Q: What types of markets do dogs and cats hate?
A: Flea-markets!

Q: What do you call a bear that is slowly losing its teeth?
A: You call it a gummy bear.

Q: What do you call a pig that practices martial arts?
A: A porkchop

Q: When a cow is caught in a tornado, what do you call it?
A: A milkshake

Q: When you see a sleeping bull, what do you call it?
A: A bulldozer

Q: Tell me the difference between climate and weather.
A: You are able to climb it but you cannot weather a tree.

Q: What does the tree wear to the summer pool parties?

A: Swimming trunks!

Q: Why did the sun go to school?
A: To get brighter!

Q: How does a ghost stay safe when he is driving?
A: He puts on his sheet belt!

Q: What do monsters turn on in the summer time?
A: Their scare conditioner!

Q: What is scarecrows' favorite food?
A: Strawberries!

Q: What kind of monster loves the disco?
A: The boogieman!

Q: Why do witches always say their name when they start a conversation?
A: So they know which witch is which!

Q: How do you make a witch itch?
A: Take away the 'W'

Q: Why is it always safe to tell a mummy your secrets?

A: Because they will keep it under wraps!

Q: Which of Santa's reindeer has an attitude problem?
A: Rude-olph!

Q: What is Frosty the Snowman's favorite type of cereal?
A: Frosted Flakes

Q: What did the hamburger name her daughter when she was born?
A: Patty!

Q: Where does Superman like to shop for food?
A: At the supermarket!

Q: A cow that has no legs is called?
A: Ground beef!

Q: What did the skeleton order for dinner?
A: Spare ribs!

Q: What is a balloon's least favorite kind of music?
A: Pop music!

Q: Why did the musician get arrested?
A: He got into some treble!

Q: What is a skeleton's favorite instrument?
A: A trombone!

Q: Which punk rock group has four men who can't sing to save their lives?
A: Mount Rushmore!

Q: What sorts of tunes do the planets listen to?
A: Nep-tunes!

Q: A bear that weighs 6,000 pounds should go where?
A: It should go dieting!

Q: Where did two walls meet?
A: On the corner!

Q: Why does a dragon always sleep from 8:00 am to 4:00 pm?
A: So they can fight knights!

Q: Cards cannot be played by pirates. Why is that?
A: Because all over the deck he walks!

Q: Two elevators are talking to each other. What did they say to each other?

A: I am not feeling good. I feel like something is coming down with me.

Q: How is a headache cured?
A: The pane will disappear if you put your head through a window!

Q: Before robbing the bank, the robber took a bath. Why is that?
A: He wants to have a clean get-a-way!

Q: What did two pencils tell one another?
A: You are looking kinda dull. Are you okay?!

Q: Why are frogs always in such a good mood?
A: They just eat whatever bugs them!

Q: What sound do porcupines make when they smooch?
A: Ouch!

Q: What did the blanket say to comfort the bed when he was upset?
A: Don't worry! I got you covered!

Q: This contains thousands of letters, ends in letter E, and begins with letter P. What do you call it?
A: A post office!

Chapter 4: Longer Dumb Jokes

George was on his way home from a party. He was walking down the street when he heard something behind him. It was making a booming noise. BOOM! BOOM! BOOM! He turned around to see a coffin following him! He started running to his house. The coffin kept following him. It got louder and louder! BOOM! BOOM! BOOM! George was frightened. Once he reached the front door of his house, he noticed the coffin right behind him. He quickly unlocked the door and tried to push the coffin out, but it followed him in any way. He ran upstairs to his bedroom and grabbed the first thing he could to throw at the coffin. A bag of cough drops. He threw them, and the coffin stopped.

"Oh no!" the kangaroo said to the snake. "We are supposed to get some rain today!"
"What is wrong with that?" said the snake. "We could use some rain. It's so dry here!"
"It just means my kids are going to have to play inside all day!" groaned the kangaroo.

A woman asked her lawyer about his fees. He told her he charges $100 for every three questions. The woman said that seems like a bit much, don't you think? He replied yes but those are my charges. He asked her what her final question was.

A little girl is sitting at home and hears a knock at the front door. She opens it and screams in disgust. It was a turtle. She throws it as far as she can and shuts the door. A year later, **she hears a knock at the door. She opens it and sees a turtle.** He asks, "What was that all about?"

A snail went to a car dealership. The salesman was very surprised that the snail wanted to buy a fast, sportscar. When the snail requested to have the sides of the car painted with a big 'S', the salesman was surprised even more. He asked the snail why he would want something like **that. The snail replied, "I want people to say, 'look at that S car go!'"**

Three men are driving through the desert when their car breaks down. They each bring an item to take on their hike into town. One of the men grabs a jug of water. The second one takes a box of crackers. The third takes the car door. One of the men says that they can drink the water in case they get thirsty. The other says they can eat the crackers in case they get hungry. The third one says he can roll down the window in case they get hot.

A father and daughter walk into a library. They both look at each other and ask the front desk clerk for two cheeseburgers and two orders of fries. The librarian looks at them and **tells them they are in a library**. The man says 'Oh' and whispers to the librarian, "We will take two cheeseburgers and two orders of fries."

A small chicken walks into a library and says, "Book, book, book!" The librarian hands the chicken a couple of small paperback books and watches as the chicken leaves the library. He walks across the street, over a hill, and disappears from the librarian's sight.
The next day the same chicken comes into the library and says, "Book, book, book!" The librarian does the same thing. She hands the chicken a few small, paperback books and watches the chicken cross the road and go over the hill. The chicken disappears from her sight again.
The day after that, the chicken walks back into the library and says, "Book, book, book!" She hands the chicken the books but instead of watching the chicken disappear, she follows it. They both cross the street and go over the hill. When they get to the other side of the hill, the librarian watches as the chicken walks up to the biggest frog she has ever seen. The chicken hands the books to the frog and he says, "Read it…read it…read it."

A son and father were sitting down for dinner. The boy turns to his dad and asks, "Dad, are bugs good to eat?"

The dad turns to his son and tells him, "Don't talk about stuff like that at dinner. That is inappropriate while we are eating!"

After the two are done eating dinner, the dad asks his son why he would ask such a question. The boy looks at his father and says, "Well, there was a big bug in your soup, but it's gone now."

Teacher: "If I gave you three cats, plus another two cats, and then another one cat. How many would you have?"

Boy: "Seven."

Teacher: "No, listen carefully. If I gave you three cats, plus two more cats, plus another cat, how many would you have?"

Boy: "Seven."

Teacher: "Okay, let me put this in a different way. If I gave you three oranges, plus two more oranges, and another one orange, how many would you have?

Boy: "Six."

Teacher: "Okay. So, if you have three cats, and I gave you two more, plus one more, how many would you have?"

Boy: "Seven."

Teacher: "No, where are you getting the number seven from?"

Boy: "I already have a cat at home!"

Mr. and Mrs. Shoe had two sons. One was named Mind Your Own Business and the other was named Trouble. The two sons decided to play a game of hide-and-seek. Trouble went to go hide while Mind

Your Own Business counted down from one hundred. Mind Your Own Business started searching for his brother everywhere. He looked underneath cars. He looked in bushes and around in a dark alley near their house. A police officer walked up to him and asked him what he was doing. "I'm playing a game," replied the brother. The policeman asked him what his name was to which the boy replied, "Mind Your Own Business." The police officer grew angry. He said, "Listen, son. Are you looking for Trouble?" Mind Your Own Business replied, "Yes. Actually, I am."

A teacher asks her students to make a sentence using the word 'beans'. One small girl spoke up and said, "My mom cooks beans at home." Another little girl stood up and said, "My father grows his own beans in our garden." A third little girl stood up and said, "We are all human beans."

A robber goes into a bank and holds everyone hostage. He says, "Give me all of your money or your chemistry!" One of the bank tellers says, "Don't you mean history?" The robber tells the bank teller, "Don't change the subject!"

Him: "Oh, no! I just fell off a 50ft ladder!"
Her: "Oh, wow! Are you okay?"
Him: "Yeah, I fell off of the first step."

One night, a queen and a king went into the castle. There was no one in the castle and no one ever came out of it. The next morning, three people walked out of the castle. Who were they? The knight, the queen, and the king.

A man was driving down the road when a policeman stopped him. When the officer approached the car, he asked the man why he had penguins in the backseat? The man replied, "These are my penguins. They belong to me." The officer said that the man needs to take them to the zoo. The next day, the police officer saw the same man driving down the road. He pulled him over to make sure he had taken the penguins to the zoo. This time, when he saw the man and the penguins, they all had sunglasses on. The police officer told him, "I thought I told you to take these penguins to the zoo?" He then replied, "I did! Today we are going to the beach!"

One person decided to pay his buddy a visit. When he arrived at his house, his mouth dropped. A dog and his friend were focused on a game of chess. The man said, "That is amazing! This has to be the smartest dog in the entire world." His friend replied. "No, not really. I've won the last three out of five games!"

A spell was put over a prince. He is only allowed to speak just a word every year. He can speak two words in a year if he doesn't speak a word the previous year, and so forth. He then met a pretty woman one day. In order for him to tell her, "my dear," he decided to not speak to her for two years. He also wants her to know that he loves her. So, before he could say anything to her, he needs to wait again for three years. After five years, he wants to ask her to marry him. So, he still needs to wait for four more years. At last, after nine years, the man can finally say, "My dear, I love you. Will you marry me?" The beautiful woman said, "I'm sorry. I didn't hear you. What?"

Connor went to go visit his 90-year old grandpa who lived far out in the country. He was going to stay for a couple of days. The first morning, his grandpa made Connor a plate full of bacon and eggs. Connor felt a weird film on the plate. He asked his grandpa if the plate was clean. His grandpa replied, "They are as clean as Cold Water can get them!" The next morning, Connor's grandpa made toast and sausage. Connor saw some left-over egg on the plate. He asked his grandpa if the plates were clean and his grandpa assured him they were. He said, "They are as clean as Cold Water can get them."

Connor was getting ready to leave his grandpa's house. When he was on his way to the front door, his grandpa's dog stopped him and began growling. Connor yelled at his grandpa, "Grandpa! Your dog won't let me leave!" His grandpa yells back, "Cold Water, go lie down! Let Connor leave."

Four men are waiting in a hospital lobby while their wives are having babies. The first nurse comes out of the room and yells at the first man. "Congratulations, you have twins!"

The man replies, "That's funny. I work for the Minnesota Twins!"

The second nurse comes out of the room and yells at the second man.

"Congratulations, you have triplets!"

The second man replies, "That's funny. I work for the 3M Company!"

The third nurse comes out of the room and yells at the third man. "Congratulations, you have quadruplets!"

The third man replies, "That's funny. I work for The Four Seasons hotel."

The last man begins crying. All of the other men look at him and ask him what is wrong.

"The last man replies, "I work for 7-Up."

The teacher asked little Bobby if he knew his numbers. He replied yes.

"Good!" the teacher says. "What comes after four?"

"Five," says Bobby.

"What about after seven?" replies the teacher.

"Eight," says Bobby.

"How about after nine?" says the teacher.

"Ten," says Bobby with a loud sigh. Bobby was growing bored of the teacher's questions.

"Okay then. What about after ten?" says the teacher.

"Jack," says Bobby.

A man comes home after a long day of work. He opens the fridge to get out a nice, cold soda. Inside, he sees a rabbit taking a little nap. The man carefully wakes up the rabbit.

He asks, "What are you doing in my fridge?"

The rabbit replies, "Isn't this a Westinghouse?"

"Uh, yes," the man replies. "It is."

"Well then," the rabbit replies, "I'm twying to west."

A businessman walked into work one morning to find that some handymen were repainting the building. He noticed that they were all wearing two windbreakers. The businessman found it a bit strange because it was a hot summer's day.

It bothered the businessman so much that he finally left his office and went to ask the handymen why they were wearing two windbreakers.

One of the handymen replied, "The can says, for best results, please use two coats."

A huge cruise ship passes by a small island. All of the passengers see a bearded man on the island running around and flailing his arms.

"Captain," one of the passengers asks, "who is that man over there on the island?"

"I have no idea," the captain replies, "but every time we drive by here, he goes crazy!"

One day, a man walks into the movie theatre with an elephant.

"I'm sorry, sir. I can't allow you to bring in an elephant to the movie theatre," says one of the managers.

"Oh, he is well-behaved! I promise," says the man.

"All right then. If you are one-hundred percent sure," says the manager.

After the movie, the manager walks up to the man. "I'm so surprised. Your elephant was so well-behaved!"

The man says, "I am, too. He hated the book!"

A small boy walked into a restaurant. He saw a sign outside that said fat-free French fries. He thought to himself that they sounded great and he was starving!

"I'll take an order of fat-free French fries," says the boy to the older gentlemen behind the counter.

"Okay, coming right up!" says the older man.

A basket of French fries was being watched by the boy as it was taken out from the fryer by the cook. When the cook placed the potatoes in a box for to-go, oil was still dripping from them.

"Hang on for a second," said the boy. "Those fries don't look fat-free."

"Sure they are," said the man. "We only charge for the potatoes. The fat is completely free."

Two dogs, a Chihuahua and a Dalmatian, were being walked by two friends. Suddenly, when they were near a restaurant, they smelled something amazing coming from it.

The man who owns the Dalmatian asks the other guy if he wants to get something to eat.

"Sure," he says, "but we have dogs with us. They won't let us in."

The guy with the Dalmatian says, "Follow my lead." After putting on a pair of sunglasses, he walked into the restaurant.

'I'm sorry, sir. You can't bring your dog in here," says the manager. "We have a strict no pets policy."

"This is my seeing-eye dog," says the man with the Dalmatian.

"A Dalmatian?" says the manager, confused.

"Yes, they are using Dalmatians now," says the man.

"Very well, then. Come on in," says the manager.

The guy with the Chihuahua follows his friends lead. He puts on some sunglasses and then walked over inside the restaurant.

The manager says, "Sorry, sir. No pets allowed."

The guy says, "but this is my seeing-eye dog."

"A Chihuahua?" says the manager.

"A Chihuahua?!" says the man. "They gave me a Chihuahua?"

Chapter 5: Kids' Puns and Other Jokes

Have you heard about the man that has his entire left side cut off? He is all right now.

My leaf blower just doesn't blow. Man, it sucks.

I'm great friends with twenty-five letters of the alphabet. I don't know why.

Somehow, I have forgotten which side the sun has risen when I woke up this morning. Suddenly, it dawned on me.

A golf ball is always going to be a golf ball. It doesn't matter how you putt it.

Can your dog do magic tricks? Mine can. He's a labracadabrador.

I tried to capture some fog. I mist.

The longer you sleep in a bed, the taller you are.

There was a boomerang joke I heard earlier, and it was really funny. I can't remember it, though. Give me a minute. It'll come back to me.

Some whiteboards are simply remarkable.

What would be the point in the end if you can make both ends of a pencil as erasers?

I was figuring out how lightning is formed as I watched a thunderstorm. Suddenly, it struck me!

A little word of advice. You should never lie to an x-ray technician. They'll always be able to see right through you.

Speed bumps are what I am extremely scared of. You shouldn't worry though. I'll get over it slowly.

I read a sales advertisement that says, "TV for sale, $1, volume stuck on full." I cannot turn that down, I thought.

Wow! That wedding was so emotional. The cake was in tiers.

Broken puppets for sale. No strings attached!

I couldn't have time to search for my lost watch.

Dead batteries were being sold on a shop I happened to pass by. There was absolutely no charge!

A long time ago, I was a soap-addict. Fortunately, I am now cleaned.

The other day, I was walking behind a clown. We both walked into the same shopping store and he opened the door for me. I thought to myself. Man, what a good jester.

The person who invented the knock-knock joke was a genius! Give that guy a no-bell prize!

I used to sing in the shower. It was great fun until I got soap in my mouth. I asked my mom how to stop it from happening. She said stop singing those soap operas.

I would like to make you laugh with my joke about construction, but I forgot the punch line. I am still working on it.

The newly bought stair lift was giving my grandma a lot of problems. It literally drives her up a wall.

I have a gift for the guy who invented the zero. Nothing!

A camouflage shirt is what I really wanted to buy. However, the right one cannot be found.

There are new reversible jackets that recently came out. Have you heard about them? How good they will turn out is a mystery.

I was figuring out how my seatbelt should be properly fastened, but it didn't work. Then it clicked!

A man just assaulted that lady with cow's milk, cheese, and some butter! How dairy!

I didn't know how I felt after my mood ring was stolen by someone.

Some food coloring was what I accidentally swallowed yesterday. When I went to the doctor, he said I was fine. I felt like I dyed a little inside.

I wondered why the baseball got bigger and bigger. And then it hit me!

Some guy was hit by a soda bottle in the head. Luckily, it was a soft drink.

These stairs cannot be trusted. They are always up to no good!

Again, my printer's making some music. I think the paper's jamming.

I saw a snake next to a Lego set the other day. I think he was a boa constructor.

My time machine and I go waaayyyy back!

The drill is known by the dentist's regular visitors.

Since she's always counting, I no longer hang out with my ex-best friend. I wonder what she is up to now!

My sister could not believe that I could make a new car made of noodles, so she made a bet of $100. The look on her face when I rode pasta was satisfying.

I have to put my foot down, finally, when I was told to stop acting a flamingo by my mom.

I have to blame my shelf when a book fell on my head.

A new type of broom came out today. People were standing in line waiting to buy it. It's really sweeping the nation!

My girlfriend quit her job at the donut factory. She was so sick and tired of the hole business.

A boiled egg in the morning is sure hard to beat.

Did you hear about the old Italian waiter? He pasta way last week.

Learning how to collect trash was difficult. I just picked it up as I went on.

My dog loves pizza. His favorite is puperoni.

Children who fail their coloring tests always need a shoulder to crayon.

The spider had to use the computer. He needed to check on his web site.

The Energizer Bunny was arrested. He was charged with battery.

"Doctor, there is a patient on line one who says he is invisible."
"Well, tell him I cannot see him right now."

I was addicted to the Hokey Pokey. Luckily, I turned myself around.

I was grateful that you explained to me the word 'many.' It means a lot.

I accidentally handed my best friend a glue stick instead of Chapstick. Now, he's not talking to me.

How did I get fired from the calendar factory, you may ask? Well, I just wanted to take a day off!

Just don't spell part backward. Trust me, it's a trap!

Did you watch the news? There was a kidnapping at the middle school. Everything is okay, though. He woke up.

A friend of mine tried to annoy me with bird buns, but I realized toucan play that game.

The bike was two-tired to stand up on its own.

If a baby refuses to sleep during nap-time, are they resisting a rest?

Chapter 6: Quirky Questions

Why does the feet smell and nose run?

If it is only happening in North America, then why do they call it The World Series?

Why is it called a building if it is already built?

If practice makes perfect, and nobody is perfect, why should they have to practice?

If a tomato is a fruit, is ketchup a smoothie?

Why is the glue not sticking inside the bottle of the glue?

If number two pencils are the most popular type of pencil, why are they called number twos?

Would seven days without exercise make one weak?

Why do you call it 'rush hour' when the traffic is slow?

Why does our hair lighten and our skin darkens when exposed to the sun?

Why does the watch's third hand call the second hand?

How much deeper would the ocean be without sponges?

How do 'stay off the grass' signs get there in the first place?

Why is it called the Secret Service if everyone knows about it?

If a mime is arrested, do the police have to tell him that he has the right to remain silent?

Why is it called a television set if you only get one TV?

Why do pizza shops put round pizzas into square boxes?

Why apartments are always built together?

Why do we drive on parkways and park in driveways?

Why is mail that gets delivered by the sea called 'CARgo' but mail delivered on land is called 'SHIPments?'

Chapter 7: Books Never Written

"How to fish" by Will Ketchum

"Healthy Foods" by Chris P. Bacon

"Living through the Storms" by Ty Foon

"Musical Instruments" by ZylaFone

"Starting a Fire" by M. Burr

"How to Win a 5k Marathon" by Sprintz A. Lott

"Architecture" by Bill Dhing

"Flying Beasts" by Tara Dactle

"Answering the Door" by Isabelle Rings

"Batman's Worst Enemy" by Joe Kurr

"Learning to Read" by Abe E. Seas

"A Guide to Flying" by Al T. Tude

"Dessert" by Sue Flay

"A Guide to New York" by Dee Big Apple

"A Detective's Case" by Mr. E.

"A Butterfly's Life" by Kat E. Pillar

"Giant Snakes" by Ann A. Conda

"How to Wrestle Bears" by Dan Jerus

"How to Work Out" by Jim Nasium

"Mathematics" by Jean Yuss

"How to be Helpful" by Linda Hand

"A Day at the Beach" by Sandy Feat

"Woodwind Instruments" by Clair E. Nett

"Everything is Going Wrong" by Mel Function

"To the Outhouse" by Willy Mayket; illustrated by Bettee Wont

"Walking to School" by Misty Bus

"Where have all of the Animals Gone?" by Darin DeBarn

"Falling off of a Cliff" by Aileen Dover N. Fell

"I was Prepared" by Justine Kase

"Green Spots on the Walls" by Picken and Flicken

"The Lost Scout" by Werram Eye

'The Bearded Man" by Harry Chin

"Crossing a Man with a Duck" by Willie Waddle

"Raise Your Arms" by Harry Pitts

"Sitting on the Beach" by Sandi C. Heeks

"My Life as a Gas Station Attendant" by Phil R. Awp

"Something Smells" by I Ben Phartin

"Household Book of Tools" by M.C. Hammer

"Late for Work" by Dr. Wages

"Computer Memory" by Meg. A. Byte

"The Future of Robotics" by Ann Droid and Cy B. Org

"What to do if you are in a Car Accident" by Rhea Ender

"Taking Tests" by B. A. Wiseman

"Over the Mountaintop" by Hugo First

Conclusion

Thank you for making through to the end of *Karen's OMG Joke Book for Kids: Funny, Silly, Dumb Jokes that Will Make Children Roll on the Floor Laughing*. Let's hope it was filled with the necessary information to make your child laugh!

This book has been written for younger kids. It isn't just the normal knock-knock jokes, although they are in the book. This book is filled with all sorts of jokes that will surely get your child laughing! There are some that will make them think. Some of them are just really bad puns that will make, even you, shake your head. There are also some classic riddles that are so popular that they've withstood the test of time. You can enjoy it as a family or leave your child to use their imagination. The book is free of dirty jokes and all jokes that use profanity. I hope you enjoyed it!

Finally, if you found this to be a good book, a review on Amazon is always appreciated!

Connect with us on our Facebook page www.facebook.com/bluesourceandfriends and stay tuned to our latest book promotions and free giveaways.

Karen's Dad Jokes

The Bad, The Funny, The Clean, And the LOL Jokes For The Cool Dad

Karen J. Bun

Table of Contents

Description

Bluesource And Friends

Introduction

Animal Jokes

Classroom and Kids' Jokes

Computer Technology Jokes

Everyday Silly Jokes and Riddles

Favorite Dad Jokes

Food Jokes

Seasonal Jokes

Knock-Knock Jokes

Occupation Jokes

Some Silly Titles of Books

Silly Slogans and Signs

Sports Jokes

Conclusion

Description

Discover the silly, clean, Laugh Out Loud jokes dad loves to tell again and again. Some of the jokes here will seem redundant, but they are all uniquely resonant to Dad who loves a good pun. Dad is a cool guy no matter what, right? We all know Dad will never pass up the opportunity to tell a corny yet funny joke. It is in their blood. They cannot help it at all. Dads will be dads, and they will always want to make us, and everyone else, laugh. This book is a celebration of dads and their innate humor. The guy who is so cool he can tell the silliest joke while appearing equally confident and in charge. It might be cheesy, but if you've ever had a dad who liked to crack a good, terrible, joke, you will appreciate all of the inclusions here.

Dad with his one-liners, what he thinks to be a clever play on words, and groan-inducing, hand-hitting-the-face hilarity, will never think to not share what he deems a funny joke. He won't just share it quietly nor elegantly either. Dad will make every effort to entice us into his provocations while thinking they are completely normal and genuinely funny. I think dad would definitely approve of the jokes here.

Some are tried and tested while others are modern and cool. This book would make a perfect Father's Day gift, birthday gift, holiday, or any special occasion to celebrate Dad gift! These are a few of the silly, banal, absurd, ridiculous, and plain old funny jokes you will read that we have all heard dad say one time or another:

- Discover new, funny animal jokes along with the classics
- Silly jokes about everyday matters, people, family, and things
- Hilarious occupation jokes
- Bad, cheesy, corny, repetitive jokes we all know, but hearing dad say them, just makes them all funnier
- Clean but funny weather and nature jokes
- Jokes and puns about famous people and events
- Laugh Out Loud sports jokes
- Downright silly book titles and authors
- Absurd holiday jokes to make you chuckle

Bluesource And Friends

This book is brought to you by Bluesource And Friends, a happy book publishing company.

Our motto is **"Happiness Within Pages."**

We promise to deliver amazing value to readers with our books. We also appreciate honest book reviews from our readers.

Connect with us on our Facebook page www.facebook.com/bluesourceandfriends and stay tuned to our latest book promotions and free giveaways.

Don't forget to claim your FREE book

https://tinyurl.com/karenbrainteasers

Also check out our best seller book

https://tinyurl.com/lateralthinkingpuzzles

Introduction

Congratulations on downloading your copy of *Karen's Dad Jokes: The Bad, the Funny, the Clean, and the LOL Jokes for the Cool Dad*. I am so glad you have decided to explore funny dad jokes for all to enjoy, young and old. Some of us may know for certain that dads and jokes go hand-in-hand. It's inevitable. Dads pretty much just have to tell jokes as soon as they officially become Dad. It is second nature; it is in their DNA. If there wasn't a dad out there who could make us laugh, chuckle, groan out loud, or shake our heads at the hilarious absurdity, then we would all be missing out. Life would not be the same without a good, bad, witty one-liner or corny jibe courtesy of good ol' dad.

Dads enjoy a cheeky pun, play on words, trite tale, or tall story or two, or three, or four. I think it must be irresistible for any dad to pass a practical joke or funny story as his own. If there is a chance to always repeat a cheesy gag or funny joke of the day, then dad is going to shine and perform the best way he knows how. His kids, co-workers, students, family, and friends may be completely embarrassed or falling over with laughter, but dad cannot and will not resist a good, silly, corny joke, especially at the expense of others. Dads themselves will admit they cannot help themselves when it comes to telling an irresistibly bad joke or pun. Everyone listening in the room can moan and roll their eyes, but dad will have the biggest grin on his face, satisfied he told yet another, really bad, joke.

This book is for the entire family to enjoy and refer to over and over again. You will find classic laughs and puns about all kinds of animals, famous people and events, nature, sports, occupations, school jokes, and more. Let dad know you appreciate him and his remarkable timing and wit by sharing these jokes with him. This book is for the young, the old, and the funny Dad of all ages!

© Copyright 2018 by Bluesource And Friends - All rights reserved.

No part of this book may be reproduced or transmitted in any form by any means, electronic or mechanical, including photocopying, recording, or by any information storage and retrieval system without written permission of the publisher, except for the inclusion of brief quotations in a review.

The following eBook is reproduced below with the goal of providing information that is as accurate and reliable as possible. Regardless, purchasing this eBook can be seen as consent to the fact that both the publisher and the author of this book is in no way experts on the topics discussed within and that any recommendations or suggestions that are made herein are for entertainment purposes only. Professionals should be consulted as needed prior to undertaking any of the actions endorsed herein.

This declaration is deemed fair and valid by both the American Bar Association and the Committee of Publishers Association and is legally binding throughout the United States.

Furthermore, the transmission, duplication, or reproduction of any of the following work including specific information will be considered an illegal act irrespective of whether it is done electronically or in print. This extends to creating a secondary or tertiary copy of the work or a recorded copy and is only allowed with an expressed written consent from the Publisher. All additional rights reserved.

The information in the following pages is broadly considered to be a truthful and accurate account of facts and as such any inattention, use, or misuse of the information in question by the reader will render any resulting actions solely under their purview. There are no scenarios in which the publisher or the original author of this work can be in any fashion deemed liable for any hardship or damages that may befall them after undertaking information described herein.

Additionally, the information in the following pages is intended only for informational purposes and should thus be thought of as universal. As befitting its nature, it is presented without assurance regarding its prolonged validity or interim quality. Trademarks that are mentioned are done without written consent and can in no way be considered an endorsement from the trademark holder.

Animal Jokes

Q: Did you hear about the paranoid bloodhound?
A: He thought everyone was following him!

Q: Where is the best place in the house to keep sled dogs?
A: In a mush room.

Q: Which dinosaur had radial wheels?
A: Tire-rannosaurus Rex.

Q: When a dog suddenly sat on sandpaper, what did it say?
A: Ruff.

Q: Phones and dogs are alike. Why?
A: Collar IDs make them both the same.

Q: When it's raining dogs and cats, what happens?
A: Stepping in a poodle is a possibility.

Q: Dogs are surely not good dancers, why?
A: Having 2 left feet is the reason why.

Q: The best time is kept by what kind of dog?
A: A watch dog.

Q: The poor dog chases his own tail. Why?
A: He wants to try to make both ends meet!

Q: Bubble baths are loved by what kind of dog?
A: It's called a shampoodoodle.

Q: A left-handed dog is called?
A: A south paw!

Q: Two fleas are talking to each other. What are they talking about?
A: Are we taking or walking a dog?

Q: The legs of a horse should be how long?
A: The ground must be reached by the horse. That's how long they should be.

Q: This type of markets is avoided by dogs. What is it?
A: Flea markets!

Q: When the cowboy's dog ran away, what did he say?
A: Well, doggone!

Q: This state has many dogs and cats. What is it?
A: Petsylvania

Q: Have you heard about the sea lions that perform?
A: I heard their reviews are wave!

Q: What is the name of the first cat that has flown an airplane?
A: Kitty-hawk

Q: The dinosaur couldn't walk, why?
A: Because it was extinct.

Q: What did Mr. Fox say when he tucked his children into bed?
A: Please have pheasant dreams.

Customer: Is that dog a good watchdog?
Pet store owner: Of course. He'll cause a ruckus every time he sees a stranger!
Customer: How do I know you are not just making that up?
Pet store owner: Because the dog comes with a money bark guarantee!

Mr. Beaver: I'm so hungry. What is for dinner?
Mrs. Beaver: A tree course meal.

Q: What's the reason the man is standing behind the horse?
A: Getting a kick out of it was what he was hoping for.

Q: Hair can be seen mostly on which horse's side?
A: The outside.

Q: A horse is scared of getting this disease. What is it?
A: Hay fever.

Q: What is the only time that a horse talks?
A: Whinney wants to!

Q: A horse that is living next door is called?
A: A neigh-bor.

Q: When the horse entered the class, what did the teacher said?
A: What's with the long face?

Q: A horse fell. What did he exclaim?
A: I couldn't giddyup after falling.

Q: A pony gargles because…?
A: It's a bit hoarse!

Q: A horse can be led to the water in this way. What is it?
A: With a lot of oats, carrots, and apples

Q: It was Friday when a man rode his horse. He, then, rode on Friday the next day. How did that happen?
A: Friday was the name of the horse.

Q: What did the hungry spider say to the other spider at the end of the week?
A: Thank goodness, it is Flyday!

Q: Why did the little girl love those talking birds so much?
A: She loved them so much because they were her grand parrots.

Q: Have you ever seen a catfish?
A: No. How did he hold the reel and rod?

Q: Why did the King of Beasts wear a cowboy hat and cowboy boots?
A: Because he wanted to do some country lion dancing.

Q: What is the reason behind the cat going to medical school?
A: He dreams of becoming a first aid kit.

Q: When going for a field trip, what is the preferred place by school kittens?
A: To the mewseum

Q: This is the best game that the cat likes playing with the mouse.
A: Catch!

Q: The song that is liked the most by a cat is?
A: Three Blind Mice.

Q: A leopard cannot hide because?
A: Because he's always spotted!

Q: Cats are good when it comes to video games. Why?
A: Having nine lives is the reason.

Q: A Red Cross-working kitten is called?
A: A first-aid Kit

Q: There is something worse than raining dogs and cats. What is it?
A: Hailing taxi cabs!

Q: The favorite color of the cat is?
A: Purrr-ple

Q: Why didn't the shark have to pay cash at the grocery store?
A: He had a credit cod with him.

Q: Why was Mrs. Rabbit so upset when I saw her earlier today?
A: Mrs. Rabbit was having a very bad hare day.

It's raining dogs and cats outside!
Yes, it is raining dogs and cats outside. I must have stepped in a hundred poodles.

Q: Why are elephants no longer allowed to swim in public swimming pools?
A: Elephants are banned from public swimming pools because they kept dropping their trunks.

Q: A charging bear can be stopped. How?
A: His credits cards should be taken away.

Q: What can adult cats have that no other creature can have?
A: Kittens

Mrs. Rabbit: How can I stay cool in the summer?
Mr. Bunny: You can always buy a good hare conditioner.

Q: What does the littlest duck in the family wear?
A: It will always wear the hand me down.

Q: What happens when fifty rabbits hop backward at the same time?
A: You get a receding hare line.

Q: What is white and black and white and black purple?
A: A violet has been stuck on the hoof of a zebra and its rolling down the hill.

Q: Differentiate a comma and a cat.
A: The end of the paws of a cat has its claws, while the end of a clause of a comma has a pause.

Q: Why did the minnow now want to go to lunch with the stork?
A: He was afraid he would get stuck with the bill.

Q: Why do lobsters not like to share?
A: Lobsters are always shellfish.

Q: Why do kangaroos make for really bad sailors?
A: Because kangaroos always jump ship.

Mr. Cockroach: Mrs. Centipede, why do you look so sad?
Mrs. Centipede: I have ten children and school starts tomorrow.

Mr. Cockroach: Most parents are excited when school starts again.
Mrs. Cockroach: Not me. All my children need new shoes!

Q: Why did the guppy join the Army's motorized vehicle division?
A: The guppy just wanted to be in a fish tank.

Classroom and Kids' Jokes

Q: Geometry teachers like what kind of lunch?
A: Square meals.

Q: 5 and 6 are scared of 7. Why?
A: Because seven ate nine.

Student: Ma'am, if there is something that I didn't do, would you be mad at me?
Teacher: No, of course!
Student: I didn't do my assignment.

Q: The mathematics book is always so sad. What do you think is the reason?
A: The reason is the many problems he has.

Q: How do you like Kindergarten, Billy?
A: I can't do anything there. I don't like it.
Q: What do you mean you can't do anything?
A: Reading and writing are foreign to me. And yet, they don't allow talking.

Q: The biology teacher didn't get married to the physics teacher because of this reason. What is it?
A: The chemistry between the two of them isn't right.

Student: My dog tried to chew up my essay homework last night.
Teacher: What did you do?
Student: I took the words right out of his mouth.

Q: Why would you bring a jump rope to school?
A: So that you can ask the principal if you can skip a grade.

Q: Who calculates how many meals are served in the cafeteria?
A: The lunch counter.

Q: Why did they evacuate the school library?
A: Because someone found dynamite in the dictionary.

Student #1: What is the difference between snow and snew?
Student #2: What's snew?
Student #1: I don't know. What's new with you?

Q: The math classroom's windowsill has a plant sitting on it. What happened to it?
A: Square roots grew from it.

Q: Where do people who play piano go to be on vacation?
A: Pianists go to the Florida Keys to be on vacation.

Q: Name the state in the entire America that is considered to be the wisest.
A: Having four As and a single B makes Alabama the smartest.

Q: It can travel all over the world despite staying in just one corner. What is it?
A: A stamp.

Teacher: What state do pencils originate from?
Student: Why, Pennsylvania, of course.

Teacher: Can you please tell me the name of the Great Plains?
Student: Sure, the F-16, Concorde, and 747.

Teacher: Where can you find the English Channel?
Student: I don't have that on my TV, so I do not know!

Q: Name the world's quickest and fastest country.
A: The fastest country in the world is Russia.

Q: Della wore this clothing. What is it?
A: Her New Jersey

Q: Washington's capital is?
A: The W!

Q: In an exam, what city cheats?
A: The cheating city is Peking

Q: What rock group has four main men but men who do not sing at all?
A: Mount Rushmore

Teacher: Do you know anything about the Dead Sea?
Student: Did it die because of sickness?

Q: What did the earthquake hear from the ground?
A: The ground said, "You crack me up!"

Q: Why is the ladder needed by the music teacher?
A: So the teacher could reach all the high notes.

Q: College isn't needed by the sun. Why?
A: Having a million degrees is the reason why.

Q: The cafeteria's clock is slow. Why?
A: It always went back four seconds.

Q: Librarians like these vegetables. What are they?
A: Quiet peas.

Q: Librarians take them when they are fishing. What are they?
A: Bookworms

Q: Name the tallest building in the world.
A: Library. It has many stories.

Q: This happened due to the invention of the wheel. What is it?
A: A revolution has happened.

Q: Can you guess how the hair of the moon was cut by the barber?
A: E-clipse it!

Q: This is what the pencil heard from the pencil sharpener. What is it?
A: Get to the point! Stop going in circles!

Q: What time do astronauts have their meals?
A: At launch time!

Q: This is considered to be the classroom's king. What object is it?
A: The ruler!

Q: This keeps the sun in the sky. What is it?
A: Sunbeams!

Q: So, how's school? Have you learned something today?
A: I still haven't learned enough. I still need to go tomorrow.

Q: This is what is taught to the elves in their school.
A: The elf-abet!

Q: The kid studied while on an airplane. Why is that?
A: Having a higher education is what he wanted.

Q: Guess what the pen said to the pencil.
A: And your point is?

Q: Getting straight A's can be easily done by…?
A: By using a ruler!

Q: The nose is scared of going to school. Why?
A: He said that getting picked on is just too much.

Q: This kind of plate is used in Venus. What is it?
A: Flying saucers

Q: Teacher: Why are you all on the floor, doing your multiplication homework?
A: Student: Because you said that tables are not allowed.

Q: What did the number eight hear from the number zero?
A: Nice belt.

Q: At school, the favorite subject of a butterfly is?
A: Mothematics.

Q: The favorite sum of a math teacher is?
A: Summer!

Q: The 2 fours don't want dinner. Why?
A: Because they already ate.

Teacher: Answer at once, whatever I ask, okay? The total of eight and two is?
Class: At once!

Q: Math teachers prefer this type of meals. What is it?
A: Square meals!

Q: The quarter didn't accompany the nickel in rolling down the hill. Why?

A: Having more cents is his reason

Teacher: I hope I don't see you looking over at David's test.
Student: I hope you don't see me either.

Q: There once was a school just for elves and dwarves. What did they do after school every day?
A: They did their gnome work together.

Q: The lesson was written by the teacher on the glass window. Why?
A: So that the lesson will be very clear.

Teacher: If $20 is given each by five people, what will you get?
Student: Oh, I will surely get myself nice shoes.

Teacher: If I had six apples in my left hand and seven oranges in my right, what would I have?
Student: You would have two big hands.

Q: It was a very sunny and hot day. Why did the teacher go to the beach?
A: Because she wanted to test the water.

Teacher: Didn't you miss school yesterday?
Student: No, not really.

Q: The teacher always had her eyes crossed. Why?
A: Because her pupils cannot be controlled!

Q: Why are the sunglasses needed by the teacher?
A: The pupils in his class are so bright!

Computer Technology Jokes

Q: What kind of food do computers snack on?
A: Micro chips.

Q: How do computers make sweaters?
A: On the interknit.

Q: Why was the computer so thin?
A: Because it didn't have enough bytes.

Government Official: Why hasn't this rocket been sent into space yet?
Science Technician: The crew is on its launch break.

Roger: Did you hear that they are planning to put 500 cattle into orbit in space?
Randy: Yes, it will be the herd shot around the world.

Computer Clerk: What do you use in turning on your computer?
Customer: My right hand
Computer Clerk: That is amazing! People mostly use the off/on button!

Systems analyst: Your computer network needs an upgrade.
Business manager: Oh, this computer can't be rid of.
Systems analyst: Your operation will be way faster when the new system is installed. Why do you want to keep this old one?
Business manager: I think it knows too much.

Customer: A twig is found on the keyboard of the computer I bought yesterday.
Store Clerk: Our apologies, sir. It's best that you talk to our branch manager.

Student: I spent the entire night on my computer.
Mother: It will be more comfortable if you're in bed.

Q: The mattress that is overstuffed is so ecstatic. Why?
A: It's spring training time!

Critic: Did you say that your new play is about launching rockets into space?
Author: Yes. It uses three stages.

Q: If you happen to see a car with a kangaroo, what do you get?
A: A self-jump-starting car.

Mr. Lightbulb: Why do you need to see a doctor?

Mrs. Lightbulb: I'm experiencing hot flashes lately.

Q: A timepiece is with a fake friend. If you happen to see them, what do you get?
A: A two-faced clock.

Q: What do you get if you cross a camera with a firefly?
A: A shutterbug with a built-in flash.

Q: During dinner, what did the little train heard from his mother train?
A: Chew, chew!

Little watch: Please help me wash my face, mom.
Mama watch: I only have two hands, wait just a sec.

Computer teacher: Why are you bringing cheese into the computer room?
Student: You told me I was going to work with a mouse today!

Q: The telephone didn't want to go back to his home. Why?
A: Because joining a three-ring circus is his dream.

Everyday Silly Jokes and Riddles

Q: Why did the gentleman go crazy in the clothing store?
A: He was told it was a good place for a fit.

Q: What country is the best place to shop for neckwear?
A: Thailand.

Q: Music is made in the head by what?
A: A head band!

Q: What did the pen hear from the paper?
A: Certainly, write on!

Q: Before stealing gold and money, the robber first took a bath. Why?
A: He needed a clean getaway.

Q: A snake's most musical part is?
A: The scales.

Q: Why is the man running around his bed?
A: He's trying to catch some sleep.

Q: How do you make a lemon drop?
A: You just drop it.

Q: The geologist heard this from the limestone. What is it?
A: Please don't take me for granite.

Q: What is bigger when it is upside down?
A: A 6.

Q: Billy went out with the prune. Why?
A: There is no date that he can find.

Q: The planets sing this kind of tune. What is it?
A: The planets sing Neptunes.

Q: The moon becomes the heaviest when?
A: During full moon.

Q: When looking for a job, this is where the seaweed goes. What is this place?
A: The kelp wanted section.

Q: How is the small flower called by the big flower?
A: Bud.

Q: What did Saturn hear from Mars?
A: Can I have a ring sometime?

Q: An ocean has this type of hair. What is it?
A: Wavy hair.

Q: You will know that the ocean is friendly by how?
A: By the way it waves.

Q: An attractive volcano is called what?
A: Lava-ble.

Q: What washes up on very small beaches?
A: Small beaches wash up microwaves.

Q: Why do you have to go to bed every evening?
A: The bed will not come to you.

Q: The music can't be listened to by the athlete. Why?
A: The record is broken because of her.

Q: Would you like to join me in a cup of tea?
A: Sure, but do you think we will both fit?

Q: When is a car door not really a car door?
A: When it's a jar.

Q: Do you know the best thing that Switzerland has?
A: There is a big plus on their flag.

Q: What did two walls say to each other?
A: See you at the corner.

Q: What is the reason behind the picture going to jail?
A: It's framed.

Q: What do toilets say to one another?
A: You look somewhat flushed.

Q: Where do an alien that weighs 500 pounds go?
A: It goes on a diet.

Q: Balloons are frightened with this type of music. What is it?
A: Balloons get scared of pop music.

Q: Why was the broom late?
A: The broom was late because it over swept.

Q: When Cinderella's pictures didn't show up, what did she say?
A: My prints will definitely come someday.

Q: During the day is the only time dragons sleep. Why?
A: They need to fight the knights.

Q: Why do bicycles always seem to fall over?
A: They are two tired.

Q: It dries up more the wetter it gets.
A: A towel.

Q: No one wants to talk to Lee, so what do you call him?
A: Lonely

Q: Were you long in the hospital?
A: No, I still have the same size.

Q: What goes ding dong and color blue?
A: An Avon lady at the North Pole

Q: What did the envelope hear from the stamp?
A: When we stick together, we can reach so many places.

Q: The laziest part of the car is called?
A: Wheels

Q: What has yellow wheels and is color green?
A: Grass. Sorry about lying about the wheels.

Q: Mickey Mouse took a trip to space. Why?
A: He is looking for Pluto.

Q: The calendar is so popular. Why?
A: It has so many dates.

Q: Your nose cannot be as long as 12 inches. Why?
A: It will become a foot.

Q: Writing with which hand is better?
A: Neither, writing with a pen is the best.

Q: What makes the newspaper different from the television?
A: Try swatting a fly using a television.

Q: April 1 makes everybody so tired. Why?
A: Finishing 31 days of March is so tiring.

Q: What is the reason that they arrested the belt?
A: Some pants were being held up by them.

Q: What did two elevators talk to each other?
A: I think I'm coming down with something!

Q: What did the impatient customer hear from the laundryman?
A: Keep your shirt on!

Q: Last night, there has been a robbery. Have you heard about it?
A: A pair of pants was held up by 2 clothespins.

Q: How can you cure a headache?
A: The pane will be gone if you put your head through a window.

Q: This object has flies and four wheels.
A: A garbage truck!

Q: The type of car that is driven by the wife of Mickey Mouse is called?
A: A minnie van!

Q: Traffic lights can't go swimming. Why?
A: Changing takes longer.

Q: It doesn't move but can go down and up. What is it?
A: Stairs

Q: Cards cannot be played by the pirates. Why?
A: Because the deck is where he was sitting.

Q: What is the reason Mozart let go of the chickens?
A: The chickens keep saying Bach, Bach, Bach!

Q: This thing is always overlooked, even by the most careful man. What is it?
A: Their nose.

Q: The cold front's opposite is called?
A: A warm back.

Q: No one believes him but everyone is listening to him. Who is he?
A: The weather reporter.

Q: How hot is it?
A: If I got steam when I turn on my lawn sprinkler, then it is so hot.

Q: When a fog disperses in California, what happens?
A: U C LA

Q: What did the lightning bolt hear from the cloud?
A: Oh, you are shocking!

Q: Hurricanes can see because of this. What is it?
A: They use their single eye.

Q: This never hits the ground whenever it falls. What is it?
A: The temperature!

Q: This bow cannot be tied. What is it?
A: A rainbow!

Q: What did two volcanoes whisper to one another?
A: I lava you!

Q: The favorite game of a tornado is called?
A: Twister!

Q: Clouds wear this kind of shorts. What is it?
A: Thunderwear shorts.

Q: What did the sports car hear from the tornado?
A: Hey, let's go for a spin!

My wife is as cold as marble. She says I take her for granite!

Mr. and Mrs. Brown had 2 children. Both of them are boys. Their names are Trouble and Mind Your Own Business. Both of them decided to play the game hide-and-seek one beautiful day. Mind Your Own Business counted from one to one hundred while Trouble was looking for a place to hide. Mind Your Own Business went searching for his brother, Trouble, in every corner, even behind bushes and trash cans. He even looked in and under the cars so that he could find him. Suddenly, a policeman went to him. He asked him what he was doing. Mind Your Own Business replied, "I'm playing a game." "What game?" The officer asked. He replied, "Hide-and-Seek." The policeman then asked for his name. He answered, "Mind Your Own Business." That made the officer furious. "Are you looking for trouble?" the policeman asked. "Yes, I am," the boy replied.

Manicurist is my mother's occupation while my dad is a dentist. Tooth and nail they fought most of their married life.

Mom said we had to keep our grocery bills down. So I bought her a paperweight.

They finally invented a computer that is as smart as a person. It puts all the blame for its mistakes on another computer.

I was thinking the entire night on what place the sun goes to when it sets. It finally dawned on me.

I always have lunch at this Japanese fast food place. You only have to take off one shoe.

There is another family that goes to the same church my family goes as well. So, one day, my nephew decided that he will make some food for them. The food was prayed over by my nephew. He then asked his son, Miguel, aged 3 years old to bless the food as well. The boy then bowed his head and prayed, "Lord God, thank you that there is still some food left for us at our home. It wasn't given to them all."

One year, during Easter, I decided to visit my granddaughter named Julie. She was 5 years old. It's a holiday so I opted to put on my best suit. I was surprised by what she said when we met. Julie said, "You look so dashing today, Granpa. You took a shower, didn't you?"

I was working in construction during the late 1950s. The corner of the house that we are leveling up was just jacked above the ground for about 4 inches. The house suddenly went down causing a loud band when one of the jacks slipped. The minister, the owner of the house, suddenly ran out. He then looked at the heavens and exclaimed, "I thought Jesus was coming." We couldn't stop laughing after that.

One afternoon, a young girl climbed and sat on the lap of her grandfather. She then asked him if she were made by God. Her grandpa replied, "Yes." She asked again, "Are you made by God, too?" The grandfather answered yes again. Then, the girl went silent while looking at the thinning hair and wrinkles of his grandfather. Suddenly, she said, "Well, I guess nowadays, he's doing a much better job."

One sweltering day, some flower seeds were being planted by a young man in his garden. It was a very sunny day because of the hot sun, making the man all sweaty. His neighbor noticed him planting and said, "I recommend that those seeds should be planted when the sun has gone down or during the morning when it is still cool." The young man smiled and replied, "Thank you. However, the package says otherwise. It said to 'Plant in full sun', so I can't do what you recommended.

There is an easier method that you can use to differentiate a vegetable and a weed when your garden needs some weeding. It is a weed if it doesn't come up after you pull on it. It is not if it easily comes out.

I have a grandson that really loves trains. His name is Michael, and he is 6 years old. One day, I challenged him to name an old steam engine's different parts. He then told me that one part is called cowcatcher. I then asked him the uses of the cowcatcher. He replied, "It is used in catching cows and scooting them of the railways so that my grandfather wouldn't have the trouble of chasing them away.

My family and I were sitting at the dining table for dinner. My sister and my wife were brainstorming on recipes. A dump cake was one of the suggestions. Honey, my daughter who is 4 years old, suddenly exclaimed, "Eww! It already has garbage in it!"

I have a son named David. He was 5 years old and still going to the daycare. One day, he came to me and announced that he didn't want to go to his school anymore. I asked him, "Why?" He said his classmates are still kids. He told me that he is already a big boy, and he can stay alone at home while I go to work. I asked him then if you will be the one to make his lunch since he can't still reach the stove. He immediately answered, "I can eat salad."

Favorite Dad Jokes

Q: How will you use 2 matchsticks to start a fire?
A: Ensure that at least one is a match.

Q: How would you go about talking with a bunch of giants?
A: You use big words!

Q: If it is not your cheese, what do you call it?
A: Nacho cheese.

Q: What do you call your dad when he falls through the ice?
A: A Pop-sicle!

Q: Getting out of it is hard but getting into is easy.
A: Trouble.

Q: In a pint, how many peas are included?
A: Only one

Q: When you say it, it breaks. What is it?
A: Silence!

Q: When is the only time that work is behind success?
A: In the dictionary!

Q: It stays in place even if it always runs. It has a round face and two hands. What is it?
A: A clock!

Q: It can still hold water no matter how many holes it has.
A: A sponge!

Q: When is the only time that the horse is behind a cart?
A: In the dictionary!

Q: It contains a million letters, ends with a letter E, and begins with a letter P. What is it?
A: Post Office!

Q: Are holes present in your shirts?
A: No.
Then how did you put it on?

Q: Does a ton of bricks weigh more than a ton of feathers?
A: No. They have the same weight.

Q: Count the number of books you can put in a backpack that is empty.
A: One!

Q: Use two letters to spell rotted.
A: DK (decay)

Q: Count the months that have 28 days.
A: All of them!

Q: If you take more away from it, it only gets bigger and bigger. What is it?
A: A hole!

Q: This never comes down, but only goes up?
A: A person's age

Small monster says to his dad: "Dad, the dentist wasn't painless like he said he would be."
Dad monster: "Did he hurt you?"
Small monster: "No, but he yelled at me when I bit his finger."

Knock-knock – "Who's there?" -- Butcher – Butcher who?
A: Butcher right foot in, butcher right foot out, butcher right foot in

and shake it all about; butcher left foot in, butcher left foot out, butcher left foot in and shake it all about!

Dad: "Hello, my name is Cliff. Why don't you drop over and come see me sometime?"

Kid: "Dad did you get a haircut?"
Dad: "No, I got them all cut."

Q: What is the reason behind the cookie crying?
A: It has been so long since his father was a wafer.

Q: How many apples grow on a tree?
A: All of them.

Dad: My son got an "A" for cutting class.
Neighbor: How could that happen? What school does he go to?
Dad: Barber school.

Q: Have you heard the roof joke?
A: Forget it. It's over your head!

Q: Count the letters in the Alphabet.
A: It contains 11 letters.

Q: Use two letters to spell cold.
A: IC

Q: Most water surrounds this state. What is it?
A: Hawaii

Q: The father of David has three boys named Crackle, Snap, and?
A: David!

Q: What will your place be in the race if you passed the man in the second place?
A: 2nd place!

Q: Name the gravity's center.
A: It's the letter V.

Q: This word in English has 3 consecutive double letters. What is it?
A: Bookkeeper

Q: This object is brown, has no legs, has a tail, and a head. What is it?
A: A penny.

Did you hear about the day the computer at the office broke down and everybody had to think?

My son wrote home from college the other day that he has grown another foot. His grandmother knit him the third sock!

The gosling never believed a word his father said. As far as he was concerned, it was all papaganda.

When the grocery store clerk asks my dad if he wants the milk in a bag, he always replies: "No, I'd like the milk in the container, please."

People are always calling me a hypochondriac. Let me tell you, it makes me sick!

Did you hear about the comedian who told the same joke three nights running? I guess he wouldn't dare tell it standing still!

I am so unlucky that I get paper cuts from get-well cards.

My sister is so lazy. She puts popcorn in the flapjack batter so the pancakes flip themselves!

A horseback riding school was recently opened by a guy. I heard the business fell off.

There are a lot of things money cannot buy. None of them are on my son's wish list.

Q: What do you call a superhero who loves ice cream?
A: A scooper-hero!

Food Jokes

Q: You can make this yummy cheese backward. What is it?
A: Edam.

Q: What is something you can never have for lunch or dinner?
A: Breakfast

Q: Name the favorite drink of a boxer.
A: Any kind of punch.

Q: What famous author wrote plays about fruit?
A: William Shakes-pear.

Q: What kind of breakfast cereal do you get when your pet bird flies into a fan?
A: Shredded tweet!

Q: Why was the oil and vinegar late for dinner?
A: Because they were dressing.

Q: What happened with the student chef who made a mess of an omelet in cooking school?
A: She was egg-spelled.

Q: What made the cookie cry?
A: Because its mother had been a wafer so long.

Q: Why did the doughnut baker close up his shop?
A: Because he was fed up with the hole business.

Q: A fake noodle's other name.
A: An impasta.

Q: There has been a race between the tomato and the lettuce. Have you heard about it?
A: The tomato was trying to catch up while the lettuce was a head.

Q: What famous author wrote poetry about French fries?
A: Edgar Allan Poe-tato.

Q: Where do smart hotdogs end up?
A: On an honor roll.

Q: Why did the potato have a black eye?
A: It got in the way of the fruit punch.

Q: This is used by the little fruit to shave itself.
A: A raisin blade.

Q: What is the worst kind of cake to have?
A: A stomachache.

Q: When the orange fell from the tree, why did it roll a little and then suddenly stop?
A: It ran out of juice.

Q: Where is the best place to find out the exact weight of the pie?
A: Way up high.

Q: What did the bored cola bottles do for excitement?
A: They played Follow the Liter.

Q: What does a seven-foot tall butcher weigh?
A: Meat.

Q: How do vegetables travel from field to field?
A: They take a taxi cabbage.

Seasonal Jokes

Q: What happened to the witch when her broomstick broke and she could no longer get around?
A: She witch-hiked.

Q: On Valentine's Day, this is what the valentine of the light bulb heard from him. What is it?
A: I love you watts and watts.

Q: What kind of plant do you get when you plant kisses?
A: You get the plant two lips.

Q: What does the Easter bunny do to stay in shape?
A: The Easter Bunny does lots of eggcercise to stay in shape.

Q: A four-leaf clover shouldn't be ironed. Why?
A: Your luck might be pressed.

Q: Where does the Easter Bunny go for breakfast?
A: The Easter Bunny goes for breakfast at IHOP.

Q: Name the favorite fruit of a scarecrow.
A: A scarecrow's favorite fruit is strawberries, of course.

Q: When will you be unlucky meeting a black cat?
A: If you're a mouse

Q: What is behind the noises in graveyards?
A: It is because of all the coffins.

Q: The road can't be crossed by the zombie? Why?
A: He has no guts.

Q: When a vampire has no mate, what is it called?
A: A bat-chelor.

Q: Why did the baby ghost seem so sad?
A: The baby ghost just wanted his mummy.

Q: What do witches put on their bagels?
A: Oh, witches put scream cheese on their bagels.

Q: What do you call a pretty witch who is also nice and friendly?
A: That's what you call failure.

Q: What did the vampire think about Dracula the movie?
A: He thought the movie was fangtastic.

Q: Why is it that vampires are hard to get along with?
A: Because they are a pain in the neck!

Q: What will you do to make the witch itch?
A: You just need to remove the w.

Q: What class is the witch's favorite subject in school?
A: Spelling.

Q: Who will be the Thanksgiving band's drummer?
A: The turkey has the drumsticks.

Q: Who doesn't feel like eating on Thanksgiving?
A: The stuffed turkey.

Q: How do you send a turkey through the mail in time for Thanksgiving?
A: You send the turkey through bird class.

Q: After getting into a fight, what happened to the turkey?
A: The stuffing got knocked out of the turkey.

Q: What is the worst kind of key to use for opening doors?
A: A Tur-key.

Q: What does the Invisible Man think of his mother and father?
A: He thinks they are a pair of transparents.

Q: What is the favorite day of the cow out of the whole year?
A: A cow is a big fan of Moo Year's Day!

Q: Why does everyone always do so poorly after Thanksgiving?
A: Because everything in the world gets marked down after the holidays.

Q: What is the Christmas song that Tarzan loved to sing?
A: Tarzan always sings Jungle Bells around Christmas.

Q: This is the preferred breakfast meal of snowmen. What is it?
A: Frosted Snow Flakes.

Q: What is the favorite Christmas song of a parent?
A: Oh, Silent Night.

Q: What is a fake stone that exists in Ireland called?
A: A sham rock.

Q: Why did Santa and his reindeer get a ticket on Christmas Eve?
A: Because their sleigh is left on a snow-parking zone.

Q: Do female deer admire Mrs. Claus?
A: Oh yes, they fawn all over her!

Q: Why is Rudolph so good at playing trivia?
A: Rudolph is good at playing trivia because he nose a lot and is very bright!

Q: Where does Santa store his suit after Christmas?
A: In the claus-it!

Q: What is an ig?
A: It is an igloo without the toilet!

Knock-Knock Jokes

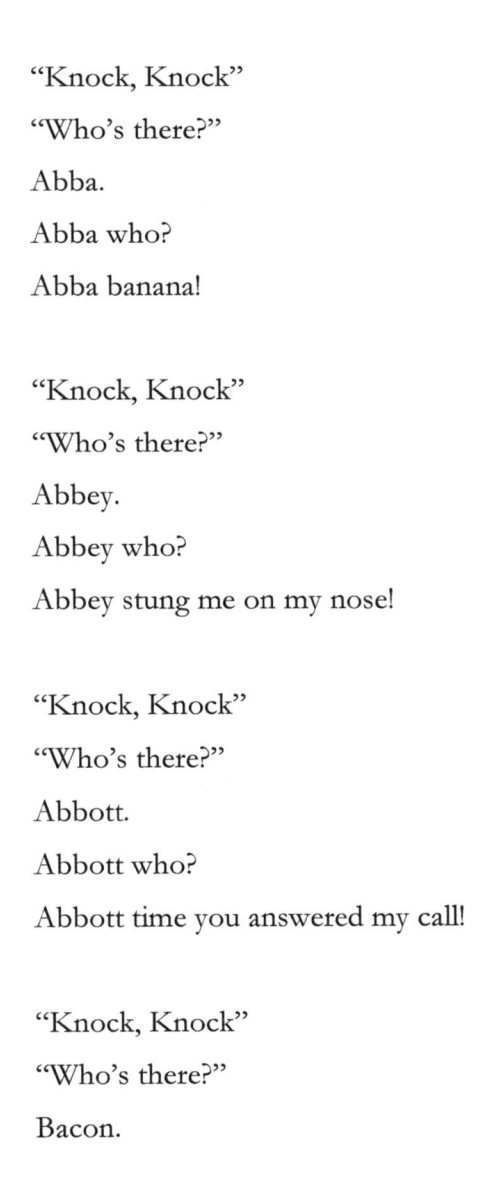

"Knock, Knock"
"Who's there?"
Abba.
Abba who?
Abba banana!

"Knock, Knock"
"Who's there?"
Abbey.
Abbey who?
Abbey stung me on my nose!

"Knock, Knock"
"Who's there?"
Abbott.
Abbott who?
Abbott time you answered my call!

"Knock, Knock"
"Who's there?"
Bacon.

Bacon who?

Bacon a pretty cake for the celebration.

"Knock, Knock"

"Who's there?"

Adam.

Adam who?

Adam up. The sum is the answer.

"Knock, Knock"

"Who's there?"

Canoe.

Canoe who?

Canoe you play this game with me?

"Knock, Knock"

"Who's there?"

Carmen.

Carmen who?

Carmen get it.

"Knock, Knock"

"Who's there?"

Carl.

Carl who?

Carl not run if you keep pressing the brakes.

"Knock, Knock"
"Who's there?"
A.C.
A.C. who?
A.C. come, A.C. go

Know, Knock
"Who's there?"
Luke
Luke who?
Luke over here and see what I'm talking about

"Knock, Knock"
"Who's there?"
Armageddon.
Armageddon who?
Armageddon happy with all these gifts?

"Knock, Knock"
"Who's there?"
Recycle
Recycle who?
Recycle around the city in our car.

"Knock, Knock"

"Who's there?"

Hank.

Hank who?

You're welcome

"Knock, Knock"

"Who's there?"

Quacker.

Quacker who?

Quacker nother joke and I'm leaving!

"Knock, Knock"

"Who's there?"

Xavier.

Xavier who?

Xavier your toys and give them to the homeless.

Occupation Jokes

Q: How is your job at the travel agency?
A: Terrible. I am not going anywhere.

Q: What do you call a person who makes miniature watches?
A: A small-time operator.

Q: Why does the custodian always wait until 11:00 a.m. to clean the floors on the weekend?
A: Because he likes to sweep late on Saturday mornings.

Q: Glasses are worn by the teacher. Why?
A: She has so many bright students.

Q: What happened to the couch potato who used to sell furniture in this store?
A: He got sacked.

Q: What kind of business did Mr. Gopher startup?
A: A hole-sale business.

Q: What is the biggest problem miners have?
A: Coal feet.

Q: An underwater spy is called?
A: James Pond!

Q: When is the time that a doctor gets mad?
A: When he runs out of patients.

Q: Who has the easiest job in the world?
A: Candle makers have the easiest job in the world. They work only on wick ends.

Q: Why was there lightning and thunder in the laboratory?
A: The scientists were brainstorming.

Q: Have you heard that gossip about the germ?
A: Forget it. I don't want that to spread out.

Q: There's a ringing sound I keep hearing, Doctor.
A: You should answer your phone.

Q: I think I'm a moth, Doctor.
A: Please get out of my light.

Q: Patient: I sometimes feel like I'm invisible, Doctor.
A: Doctor: Who said that?

Q: What did two tonsils say on each other?
A: Get dressed up, the doctor is taking us out!

Q: When a boat is sick, where does it go?
A: To the dock!

Q: Why did the doctor lose his temper?
A: Because he has no patients anymore.

Q: The pillow went to the doctor's office. Why?
A: He was feeling all stuffed up!

Q: Why did the cookie feel like it had to go to the hospital?
A: Sadly, the cookie was feeling a little crummy.

Q: How do put the baby of an astronaut to sleep?
A: You rocket.

Q: An actor fell through the floorboards.
A: He was just going through a stage.

Q: What award did the dentist get?
A: A little plaque

Q: Does your tooth still hurt?
A: I'm not sure, the dentist kept it.

Q: What is the favorite animal of a dentist?
A: A molar bear.

Q: What did the dentist hear from the tooth when it was leaving?
A: When you get back, fill me in.

Q: When there is an earthquake, what does the dentist do?
A: She braces herself!

Q: This is the best time to visit a dentist.
A: Tooth-Hurty.

Q: The king went to the dentist. Why?
A: He wants his teeth crowned.

Q: The tree went to the dentist. Why?
A: He wants his root canal removed.

Q: What did the dentist hear from the judge?
A: Do you swear to pull the tooth, the whole tooth, and nothing but the tooth?

Q: What did two teeth say to each other?
A: Thar's gold in them fills.

Q: Why did the nurse carry around a red pen?
A: So she could draw blood.

Q: Did you hear that the farmer down the road is not going to grow carrots any longer?
A: He said the carrots are long enough.

Q: A nurse walked into the busy office of the doctor and said, "Doctor, the Invisible Man is here."
A: "Sorry, I can't see him," replied the doctor.

Customer: My watch only runs every other day.
Salesperson: It was probably made by a part-time employee.

Q: What is the favorite song of all electrical engineers?
A: Ohm on the Range

Reporter: What is it like to be an astronaut?
Astronaut: It is a little weird. It is really the only job in the world where you get fired before you go to work.

Q: If an athlete's foot is for athletes, then what is for astronauts?

A: Missile toe.

Mr. Crow: I do not really feel like going to work today!
Mrs. Crow: Well, caw in sick.

Q: The favorite day of the week of a monk is?
A: Friarday.

Q: Why was the catamaran boat so upset?
A: He was docked a day's pay.

Sam: Hello Jerry! I haven't seen you in ages. How is your business?
Tom: Oh, it couldn't be better, Sam. I am always looking at piles of money!
Sam: Really, how do you do it?
Tom: I'm a bank teller.

Harry: You should really hire Joe to represent you in your lawsuit.
Mary: Joe? Why him? He graduated at the bottom of his law school class. I don't think he has ever won a case.
Harry: True, but he will lose for you cheaper than anyone else in town.

Boss: You never do some work and yet you want a raise? You've got the nerve!

Employee: Let's just say that the others have no extra burden when I went on a vacation.

Q: How is the job going?
A: I had to quit due to illness and fatigue.
Q: Oh. The boss was sick and tired of you, huh?

Mr. Green: Why is the chimney sweep so happy?
Mr. White: It's flue season!

Reporter: Can you tell me about your tennis ball company not doing well?
Business person: Yes. It will bounce back.

Some Silly Titles of Books

Don't Leave Without Me by Isa Coming

Tape Recording for Beginners by Cass Ette

The Terrible Problem by Major Setback

My Golden Wedding by Annie Versary

A Call for Assistance by Linda Hand

Water Garden Features by Lily Pond

Will He Win? By Betty Wont

Making the Least of Life by Minnie Mumm

Making the Most of Life by Maxie Mumm

Truthful Tales by Frank Lee

The Haunted Room by Hugo First

The Winning Game by Vic Tree

Beginning Magic by Beatrix Star

Dangerous Germs by Mike Robes

Grand Canyon Adventures by Rhoda Donkey

The Garlic Eater by I. Malone

How to Make Money by Robin Banks

Hide and Seek by I.C. Hugh

Season's Greetings by Mary Christmas

The Wrong Shoe by Titus Canbe

The Ghost of a Witch by Eve L. Spirit

Reaching the Top by Ella Vator

Boo! By Terry Fied

My Crystal Ball by C.A. Lot

Making Enemies to Lose Friends by Olive Alone
Heat Your House in Winter by Ray D. Ater

Silly Slogans and Signs

Repeated with pride by all of the most observant Dads!

Picture Frame Store: We want to hang around your house.

Rope Company: If you can't afford a clothes dryer, inquire about a credit line.

Thermostat Company: Install one of our thermostats, and you'll never have to worry about your home cooking.

Famous Glue Company: Customers always stick with us.

Furnas Company: We are proud to be full of hot air.

Shoelace Company: We are truly fit to be tied.

Rope Inc.: Knot your ordinary company.

On a honey farm: You will like our grade of honey. It's bee plus!

In a bankrupt bakery: No dough!

On a rodeo gate: Bronc riders needed immediately, big bucks possible!

In the window of a pillow and comforter store: For sale – all it takes is a small down payment.

In the window of a health food restaurant: All you should eat: $3.50

In the gym's window: The weak ends here!

On the door of a police detective: Out to hunch.

In a cheese plant: We never lie about our aging.

In a bowling alley: Win some pin money when you sign up for our cash prize tournament.

Tire Company: Our tires will give your car good traction on wet roads. We skid you not!

On a travel agency: When we say that we want you to go away, we mean it!

In a fish factory: Many are cod, but few are frozen.

Sports Jokes

Q: Why does the baseball stadium always feel cold?
A: Because it is full of fans.

Q: When a baseball pitcher throws, why does he raise one leg?
A: When both of his legs are raised, he would fall.

Q: What job did Dracula get with the Transylvanian baseball team?
A: Bat boy.

Q: Why is bowling a quiet sport?
A: A pin drop can be heard.

Q: Where do football players dance?
A: At a foot ball.

Q: The fans of the Brazilian soccer are called what?
A: Brazil nuts!

Q: Why does a polo player ride a horse?
A: Because they are too heavy to carry.

Q: The favorite teams of hens are encouraged by how?
A: They keep on egging on them.

Q: Who won the race between two balls of string?
A: They were tied.

Q: Baseball games aren't liked by grasshoppers. Why?
A: Cricket is their preferred game.

Q: When we play a game with big cats, why do we need to be careful?
A: They might be cheetahs.

Q: What is the favorite color of a cheerleader?
A: Yeller.

Q: Name the skydiving's hardest part?
A: The ground!

Q: Why did the man keep doing the backstroke?
A: Because his stomach is so full after eating so much.

Q: Magicians and hockey players have this similarity. What is it?
A: The two of them do hat tricks!

Q: What is the favorite sport of an insect?
A: Cricket!

Q: Why did the ballerina quit?
A: Because it was tu-tu hard!

Q: Tarzan loves spending time on a golf course. Why?
A: He wants to perfect his swing.

Q: Tennis is a really loud sport. Why?
A: A racquet is raised by the players.

Q: The faster you ran, the harder it is to catch. What is it?
A: Your breath

Q: Why did the football coach go to the bank?
A: The coach wants to have his quarter back.

Q: To stay cool, baseball players do this. What is it?
A: They sit next to the fans.

Q: Waiters is very good in what kind of sport?
A: Tennis, since they are good at serving.

Q: When it comes to hitting a baseball, what animal is the best?
A: A bat!

Q: The favorite letter of a golfer is?
A: Tee!

Q: What is the similarity between a pancake and a baseball team?
A: A good batter is what they both need.

Q: Why are two pairs of pants worn by the golfer?
A: In case he got a hole in one!

Q: A basketball-playing pig is called?
A: A ball hog.

Q: Donuts are loved by basketball players. Why?
A: Because they can dunk them.

Q: What is the reason why the basketball player is sent to jail?
A: The ball is shot because of him.

Q: What time is the baby good at basketball?
A: When the baby is dribbling.

Q: Soccer can't be played by Cinderella. Why?
A: She always runs away from the ball.

Q: What is the favorite food of a cheerleader?
A: Cheerios.

Q: What are four bullfighters that are in a quicksand called?
A: Quattro sinko.

Q: A not working boomerang is called?
A: A stick.

Q: The favorite position of a ghost in soccer is called?
A: Ghoul keeper.

Conclusion

Thank you so much for making it through to the end of this book. I hope it was informative and able to provide you with all of the tools you need to learn about, tell, and share funny dad jokes. The next step is to start trying out some of the jokes described here in your own life. Practice reading them out loud. Try to memorize them. If you are able to, talk to your own dad and see what jokes are funniest to him. If you are a dad yourself, you might try some of these out on your friends, family, co-workers, or your own kids. If you have a dad, try your hand at making him laugh at the banal and absurd. See if you can make him laugh as much as he can make you and others laugh, hand to forehead groan, and eye roll with a head shake. Experience familiar and famous puns repeated in their own unique manner here within the intimacy of your own family. These jokes should make you laugh, celebrate, and agree that dads and silly, pun-tastic jokes go hand-in-hand. We don't always know what makes Dad tick, but we do know he has the time of his life starting the day with a good joke, pranking his best friend, or embarrassing his kids over and over again. Have fun with the jokes in this book. Say them aloud to your best friend, teacher, or dad himself. Celebrate Dad with his innate ability and desire to make light of anything and everything. It is just what dads do. We love them all the more for it. If you enjoyed this book, please take the time to rate it on Amazon. Your honest review would be greatly appreciated. Thank you!

Connect with us on our Facebook page www.facebook.com/bluesourceandfriends and stay tuned to our latest book promotions and free giveaways.

Karen J. Bun

Karen's Knock Knock Jokes for Kids

The Unbreakable Door That No One Ever Got Past

Karen J. Bun

Table of Contents
Bluesource And Friends 166

Introduction.. 168

Knock knock jokes!.. 171

Conclusion 393

Bluesource And Friends

This book is brought to you by Bluesource And Friends, a happy book publishing company.

Our motto is **"Happiness Within Pages."**

We promise to deliver amazing value to readers with our books.

We also appreciate honest book reviews from our readers.

Connect with us on our Facebook page www.facebook.com/bluesourceandfriends and stay tuned to our latest book promotions and free giveaways.

Don't forget to claim your FREE book

https://tinyurl.com/karenbrainteasers

Also check out our best seller book

https://tinyurl.com/lateralthinkingpuzzles

Introduction

Knock knock jokes have been around for ages bringing delight and joy to those who hear them every day. Children giggle, have fun, and feel closer or connected to the person telling the joke and often repeat it for all their friends to hear because they believe it is so funny. They can make people laugh after a hard day or cheer someone up when they are sick or feeling down. They have been around since about the early twentieth century, and they are a staple of American humor. The great thing about these jokes is they can be understood by kids and adults alike. No matter your age there is a knock knock joke out there for you, and even if there isn't, you'll still be able to grasp the concept of each one. This makes it great for people of all ages to feel closer to each other and laugh together.
As they began to gain popularity, they could be heard just about everywhere with people making up new jokes every day. Businesses even held knock knock joke contests because they became so popular and had people flocking to them. Some orchestras even added knock knock jokes into their musical set. Radio stations would also play jokes on the air. There were some that during political campaigning times would play all day. It was everywhere you turned around. Grocery stores even printed them in their ads to drum up business because the jokes were gaining so much attention with the masses and they wanted more people to come to them. Soon after the craze

started, knock knock clubs arose and soon after people began singing songs about knock knock jokes as well. It's even been guessed that Shakespeare wrote a few knock knock jokes in his plays. Some of them appeared in his most famous plays.

They did lose traction for a little while during certain political campaigns, and it looked like they might be phased out as a negative stigma arrived from knock knock jokes. Fortunately, they weren't, and the jokes lived another day with books beginning to fly off the shelves again at bookstores or library shelves as people began to read and discover them again. Once this happened, people realized that while they were popular, it was still hit or miss. This makes sense because everyone is different and has their own sense of humor. So, there are some that like them and some that are still skeptical about the scale of their funniest jokes.

A knock knock joke for those that don't know is a question and answer joke. Mostly for kids these days there are a few exceptions. Basically, what happens is you ask a question, and then they answer. You add your answer and then finish the joke. Versatile as they are funny, knock knock jokes can be told at any occasion because there are jokes for every holiday from Christmas to Halloween or Thanksgiving and there are jokes for every occasion. You can make knock knock jokes about animals, food, life, jobs, or teachers. You can make up knock knock jokes on any subject. They've been put in everything from books to movies, and whether you're a fan of the knock knock joke or not, they're here to stay. Authors have sold millions of books on knock knock jokes because children love them so much and most people are fans and think they're absolutely delightful and funny.

This book covers a variety of topics with our jokes to make you laugh out loud and have fun while reading which is a win-win on both accounts. This also helps children who don't necessarily like reading. Most children like to read things that make them laugh and get them interested. This is why we have chosen so many different topics of knock knock jokes for this particular book.

Knock knock jokes!

Knock knock,
Who's there?
I.
I who?
I am here!!!

Knock knock,
Who's there?
You.
You who?
You are here!!!!

Knock knock,
Who's there?
Be.
Be who?
Be yourself.

Knock knock,
Who's there?
You.
You who?

I see you!!

Knock knock,

Who's there?

Me.

Me who?

You see me!

Knock knock,

Who's there?

Owl.

Owl who?

Hoo hoo hoo hoo!

Knock knock,

Who's there?

I.

I who?

I love you!

Knock knock,

Who's there?

Moo.

Moo who?

Cows go moo!

Knock knock,

Who's there?

Atch.

Atch who?

Bless you, sweetie.

Knock knock,

Who's there?

Love.

Love who?

I love you.

Knock knock,

Who's there?

Pee.

Pee who?

Peekabo, I see you!!

Knock knock,

Who's there?

Beat.

Beat who?

Let's keep the beat going on and on!

Knock knock,

Who's there?

Who's there?

Happy.

Happy who?

Knock knock,

Who's there?

Lion.

Lion who?

Don't be lion to me, mister!

Knock knock,

Who's there?

Adore.

Adore who?

I adore you!

Knock knock,

Who's there?

Bee.

Bee who?

Honeybees!

Knock knock,

Who's there?

None.

None who?

None of your business.

Knock knock,

Who's there?

Remember.

Remember who?

Remember me!

Knock knock,

Who's there?

Thank you.

Thank you who?

Thank you for being my best friend.

Knock knock,

Who's there?

Ready.

Ready who?

Ready set goes!!

Knock knock,

Who's there?

Alphabet.

Alphabet who?

Alphabet soup!

Knock knock,

Who's there?

How.

How who?

How are you?

Knock knock,

Who's there?

Miss.

Miss who?

Do you miss me because I miss you!

Knock knock,

Who's there?

Me.

Me who?

Me standing right here, can't you see me?

Knock knock,

Who's there?

Karate.

Karate who?

Karate chop!

Knock knock,

Who's there?

Wanna.

Wanna who?

You wanna play hide and seek?

Knock knock,

Who's there?

Ho ho.

Ho ho who?

No no no. It's ho ho ho!

Knock knock,

Who's there?

Stuck.

Stuck who?

The door is stuck I can't see you.

Knock knock,

Who's there?

Love.

Love who?

Do you love me because I love you!

Knock knock,

Who's there?

Cashew.

Cashew who?

Do you like Cashews? I like walnuts.

Knock knock,

Who's there?

Live.

Live who?

I'm your new neighbor. I live right next to you.

Knock knock,

Who's there?

Untied.

Untied who?

Your shoelaces untied.

Knock knock,

Who's there?

May I.

May I who?

May I borrow a pen?

Knock knock,

Who's there?

You can.

You can who?

You can come play with us if you want to.

Knock knock,

Who's there?

Who.

Who who?

Who who we've got an owl in the house!

Knock knock,

Who's there?

Forget.

Forget who?

Forget no one remember us all.

Knock knock,

Who's there?

Gotta.

Gotta who?

I gotta go my momma is calling me.

Knock knock,

Who's there?

Remember.

Remember who?

Remember me silly!

Knock knock,

Who's there?

Sure do.

Sure do who?

I sure do love you.

Knock knock,

Who's there?

Bite.

Bite who?

You're supposed to bite your food first then you chew it.

Knock knock,

Who's there?

Outside.

Outside who?

I've been outside looking for you.

Knock knock,

Who's there?

Cold.

Cold who?

I'm cold out here waiting for you.

Knock knock,

Who's there?

Where.

Where who?

Where are you?

Knock knock,

Who's there?

I can.

I can who?

I bet I can tell more knock knock jokes than you.

Knock knock,

Who's there?

Please.

Please who?

Please come with me. It will be no fun without you.

Knock knock,

Who's there?

Whatcha.

Whatcha who?

Whatcha doing today?

Knock knock,

Who's there?

Holly.

Holly who?

Happy holidays to you!

Knock knock,

Who's there?

How.

How who?

How do you know who's knocking?

Knock knock,

Who's there?

School.

School who?

Is there school today?

Knock knock,

Who's there?

Halloween candy.

Halloween candy who?

You have all the Halloween candy with you.

Knock knock,

Who's there?

Treat.

Treat who?

Trick or treat. It's Halloween!

Knock knock,

Who's there?

Wrong.

Wrong who?

I got the wrong door.

Knock knock,

Who's there?

Present.

Present who?

Open up. I have a present for you!

Knock knock,

Who's there?

I see.

I see who?

I can see you. Let me in to play with you.

Knock knock,

Who's there?

I win.

I win who?

I win, so you lose.

Knock knock,

Who's there?

Dino.

Dino who?

Dinosaur roar!!!

Knock knock,

Who's there?

Hug.

Hug who?

Hug me so I can hug you!

Knock knock,

Who's there?

Shhh.

Shhh, who?

Shhh, it's a secret. Don't let them hear you.

Knock knock,

Who's there?

Wish.

Wish who?

I wish you a Merry Christmas and a happy one too.

Knock knock,

Who's there?

I say.

I say who.

I say so that is who.

Knock knock,

Who's there?

Salt.

Salt who?

Salt goes with pepper.

Knock knock,

Who's there?

How.

How who?

How are you doing today?

Knock knock,

Who's there?

Fine.

Fine who?

Oh, I am fine today, how are you?

Knock knock,

Who's there?

Any.

Any who?

Is anybody home today?

Knock knock,

Who's there?

Tell.

Tell who?

Tell them to let me in.

Knock knock,

Who's there?

Be.

Be who?

Beware because it's Halloween today.

Knock knock,

Who's there?

Shock.

Shock who?

Are you shocked to see me because I am shocked to see you!

Knock knock,

Who's there?

I'll.

I'll who?

I'll give you a hug if you give me one too.

Knock knock,

Who's there?

Lean.

Lean who?

Lean a little closer, I have a secret for you.

Knock knock,

Who's there?

Partridge.

Partridge who?

Have a partridge in a pear tree.

Knock knock,

Who's there?

Jolly.

Jolly who?

He's a jolly good fellow.

Knock knock,

Who's there?

Don't.

Don't who?

Don't you know it's me at the door?

Knock knock,

Who's there?

Hide.

Hide who?

Hide and go seek!

Knock knock,

Who's there?

Tag.

Tag who?

Tag your it!

Knock knock,

Who's there?

Know.

Know who.

You know me the best.

Knock knock,

Who's there?

Mom.

Mom who?

It's your mom let me inside.

Knock knock,

Who's there?

Terrific.

Terrific who?

Have a terrific day today!

Knock knock,

Who's there?

Tissue.

Tissue who?

Tissues for you as you keep sneezing.

Knock knock,

Who's there?

Scream.

Scream who?

I will scream if I can't play with you.

Knock knock,

Who's there?

Chance.

Chance who?

Any chance of you letting me in soon?

Knock knock,

Who's there?

Terrible.

Terrible who?

I feel terrible when I can't see you.

Knock knock,

Who's there?

Have we.

Have we who?

Have we been here before?

Knock knock,

Who's there?

Miss.

Miss who?

I know you miss me, I miss you too.

Knock knock,

Who's there?

Bet.

Bet who?

I bet you couldn't tell it was me.

Knock knock,

Who's there?

Locked.

Locked who?

The door is locked, so I can't play with you.

Knock knock,

Who's there?

Anybody.

Anybody who?

Isn't anyone going to let me in?

Knock knock,

Who's there?

Me.

Me who?

You still don't remember me?

Knock knock,

Who's there,

Excited.

Excited who?

Are you excited to see me today?

Knock knock,

Who's there?

Here.

Here who?

Here is another good knock knock joke for you.

Knock knock,

Who's there?

Thank you.

Thank you who?

Thanks for letting me in today.

Knock knock,

Who's there?

Secret.

Secret who?

I can't tell you, or it won't be a secret.

Knock knock,

Who's there?

Three.

Three who?

There are three bunnies in your kitchen.

Knock knock,

Who's there?

Come on.

Come on who?

Come on outside and play.

Knock knock,

Who's there?

Glad.

Glad who?

Aren't you glad it's finally the weekend?

Knock knock,

Who's there?

Great.

Great who?

I had a great time with you.

Knock knock,

Who's there?

Hurry.

Hurry who?

Can you hurry and let me in, please?

Knock knock,

Who's there?

Wonderful.

Wonderful who?

It has been so wonderful to see you.

Knock knock,

Who's there?

Hippo.

Hippo who?

Hippopotamus!!

Knock knock,

Who's there?

How.

How who?

How are you today?

Knock knock,

Who's there?

Why.

Why who?

Why is it always me knocking on the door?

Knock knock,

Who's there?

Ran.

Ran who?

I ran all the way here to tell you this knock knock joke.

Knock knock,

Who's there?

Sore.

Sore who?

My hand is sore from all this knocking I'm doing.

Knock knock,

Who's there?

Bell.

Bell who?

Is your bell working? I can't hear it.

Knock knock,

Who's there?

Cry.

Cry who?

I am going to cry because I want to see you.

Knock knock,

Who's there?

Car.

Car who?

I have a new car! Now I can come to see you.

Knock knock,

Who's there?

Glasses.

Glasses who?

Can you see me, or did you forget to wear your glasses?

Knock knock,

Who's there?

Neighbors.

Neighbors who?

We are neighbors now, we can always play.

Knock knock,

Who's there?

Dinner.

Dinner who?

You're just in time for dinner.

Knock knock,

Who's there?

Mind.

Mind who?

Would you mind letting me in?

Knock knock,

Who's there?

Dog.

Dog who?

You have a dog inside, I can hear him!

Knock knock,

Who's there?

Guess.

Guess who?

Did you guess it was me at your door?

Knock knock,

Who's there?

Kangaroo.

Kangaroo who?

I have a kangaroo that wants to play with you.

Knock knock,

Who's there?

Look.

Look who?

Surprise look who is at your door.

Knock knock,

Who's there?

Picnic.

Picnic who?

Let's go on a fun picnic.

Knock knock,

Who's there?

Look.

Look who?

Look who came all the way to see you!

Knock knock,

Who's there?

Question.

Question who?

I have a question for you.

Knock knock,

Who's there?

Awesome.

Awesome who?

Awesome day for these knock knock jokes, right?

Knock knock,

Who's there?

Ignore.

Ignore who?

You ignored me knocking on your door.

Knock knock,

Who's there?

Best friend.

Best friend who?

It's your best friend who has come to see you!

Knock knock,

Who's there?

Mind.

Mind who?

Will you make up your mind and let me in, please?

Knock knock,

Who's there?

Eat.

Eat who?

Do you know a good place to eat, I am starving?

Knock knock,

Who's there?

Nice.

Nice who?

It's been so nice to see you today.

Knock knock,

Who's there?

None.

None who?

It's none of your business, that's who.

Knock knock,

Who's there?

Grandma.

Grandma who?

It's your grandma opens the door.

Knock knock,

Who's there?

Grandpa.

Grandpa who?

Now you know grandma didn't come without grandpa.

Knock knock,

Who's there?

Bell.

Bell who?

Your bell is broken. We will knock instead.

Knock knock,

Who's there?

Know.

Know who?

Don't worry I know plenty of jokes to tell you.

Knock knock,

Who's there?

Sick.

Sick who?

Are you sick of these knock knock jokes yet?

Knock knock,

Who's there?

More.

More who?

More knock knock jokes coming your way.

Knock knock,

Who's there?

Kiss.

Kiss who?

Kiss me!

Knock knock,

Who's there?

Silly.

Silly who?

Why all the silly questions today?

Knock knock,

Who's there?

Cookie.

Cookie who?

I have a cookie. I will share it with you.

Knock knock,

Who's there?

Sad.

Sad who?

I am sad you won't invite me in.

Knock knock,

Who's there?

Police.

Police who?

Let's play police officer!

Knock knock,

Who's there?

Soda.

Soda who?

Can you fill my glass with soda, please?

Knock knock,

Who's there?

Pass.

Pass who?

I thought I would pass by and see you today.

Knock knock,

Who's there?

Pass.

Pass who?

Can you please pass the chicken?

Knock knock,

Who's there?

Mother.

Mother who?

You want to play mother. May I too?

Knock knock,

Who's there?

Pants.

Pants who?

You put on your pants first and then your shoes.

Knock knock,

Who's there?

Quiet.

Quiet who?

You have to be quiet. It's a library.

Knock knock,

Who's there?

Quack quack.

Quack quack who?

Quack quack! The ducks want to play with you.

Knock knock,

Who's there?

Tell.

Tell who?

If you tell another bad knock knock joke, I am leaving.

Knock knock,

Who's there?

Dance.

Dance who?

Get up and let's dance around the room.

Knock knock,

Who's there?

Bark.

Bark who?

Your dog is barking. Can't you hear him?

Knock knock,

Who's there?

Bark.

Bark who?

Bark, bark, bark! Your puppy wants to play with you.

Knock knock,

Who's there?

Remember.

Remember who?

You remember me, don't you?

Knock knock,

Who's there?

Time.

Time who?

I am on time today to see you.

Knock knock,

Who's there?

Hungry.

Hungry who?

I am hungry, how about you?

Knock knock,

Who's there?

Sorry.

Sorry who?

Oh sorry, I have the wrong house.

Knock knock,

Who's there?

Nice.

Nice who?

Nice of you to invite me in, thank you.

Knock knock,

Who's there?

Questions.

Questions who?

You ask a lot of questions.

Knock knock,

Who's there?

Phone.

Phone who?

Can I borrow your phone, I need to call home?

Knock knock,

Who's there?

Hungry.

Hungry who?

Hungry hippos!

Knock knock,

Who's there?

Tall.

Tall who?

Not me, I can't reach the doorbell.

Knock knock,

Who's there?

Stop.

Stop who?

Can you stop and let me in, please?

Knock knock,

Who's there?

Who.

Who, who?

Did anyone hear that owl?

Knock knock,

Who's there?

Green.

Green who?

You are turning green. Are you alright?

Knock knock,

Who's there?

Thank.

Thank who?

Thank you for being awesomely you!

Knock knock,

Who's there?

Five.

Five who?

Did you know that five plus five makes ten?

Knock knock,

Who's there?

All.

All who?

All of us are the best of friends.

Knock knock,

Who's there?

Scared.

Scared who?

I am not scared, are you?

Knock knock,

Who's there?

Truth.

Truth who?

Truth or dare?

Knock knock,

Who's there?

Bell.

Bell who?

Try the bell instead of knocking.

Knock knock,

Who's there?

Utterly.

Utterly who?

Utterly funny these knock knock jokes are.

Knock knock,

Who's there?

Told.

Told who?

I told you, you have to knock first.

Knock knock,

Who's there?

I'll be.

I'll be who?

Anyone you want to be.

Knock knock,

Who's there?

There.

There who?

I'll be there for you.

Knock knock.

Who's there?

There.

There who?

You're over there, I can see you.

Knock knock,

Who's there?

When.

When who?

Do you know when mom is coming home?

Knock knock,

Who's there?

Would.

Would who?

Would you like to know who came to see you?

Knock knock,

Who's there?

Would.

Would who?

Would you like to play with me today?

Knock knock,

Who's there?

Won't you?

Won't you who?

Won't you listen to some more knock knock jokes?

Knock knock,

Who's there?

Big foot.

Big foot who?

Oh my gosh did you see big foot too!

Knock knock,

Who's there?

When.

When who?

When are you gonna answer the door for me?

Knock knock,

Who's there?

Alone.

Alone who?

Will you play with me, so I'm not alone?

Knock knock,

Who's there?

Eggs.

Eggs who?

Let's have eggs for breakfast today.

Knock knock,

Who's there?

Excited.

Excited who?

Are you excited to see me because I am to see you?

Knock knock,

Who's there?

You.

You who?

You get to come over and play with me today.

Knock knock,

Who's there?

You.

You who?

You go first, and I will follow right behind you.

Knock knock,

Who's there?

Who?

Who, who?

Who did you expect to be here at your door?

Knock knock,

Who's there?

Any.

Any who?

Is anybody home?

Knock knock,

Who's there?

Cute.

Cute who?

You're so cute!

Knock knock,

Who's there?

Explain.

Explain who?

Can you explain it to me? I don't understand.

Knock knock,

Who's there?

Teacher.

Teacher who?

My mom's a teacher. What does your mom do?

Knock knock,

Who's there?

Little.

Little who?

I am just a bunny rabbit. How would I know such things?

Knock knock,

Who's there?

Need.

Need who?

I think I need a nap. How about you?

Knock knock,

Who's there?

Night time.

Night time who?

It's night. It's bedtime for you.

Knock knock,

Who's there,

Big.

Big who?

I'm a big girl now.

Knock knock,

Who's there?

Kiss.

Kiss who?

Kiss grandma and give her a hug too.

Knock knock,

Who's there?

Pants.

Pants who?

Silly guy, my pants won't fit you.

Knock knock,

Who's there?

Bed.

Bed who?

It's past your bedtime.

Knock knock,

Who's there?

Socks.

Socks who?

Socks go on first. Then you can put on your shoes.

Knock, knock,

Who's there?

Tie.

Tie who?

If you can't tie your own shoes, I can help you.

Knock knock,

Who's there?

Walk.

Walk who?

I'd walk a hundred miles just to see you.

Knock knock,

Who's there?

Al.

Al who?

Alligator!

Knock knock,

Who's there?

Pack.

Pack who?

I'll pack the car up for you.

Knock knock,

Who's there?

See.

See who?

See you later sweetie.

Knock knock,

Who's there?

Coo coo.

Coo coo who?

I'm not coo coo silly.

Knock knock,

Who's there?

Starving.

Starving who?

Do you have anything to eat? I am starving.

Knock knock,

Who's there?

Go.

Go who?

If you go to the door, I am here to see you.

Knock knock,

Who's there?

Grill.

Grill who?

Can you grill me a burger?

Knock knock,

Who's there?

Bug.

Bug who?

Oh, I am sorry am I bugging you?

Knock knock,

Who's there?

Thump.

Thump who?

Thump thump. We're bunny rabits today!

Knock knock,

Who's there?

Bee.

Bee who?

Watch out there's a bee on you.

Knock knock,

Who's there?

Reach.

Reach who?

Reach out and hug someone today.

Knock knock,

Who's there?

Tail.

Tail who?

Please don't pull the dog's tail sweetie.

Knock knock,

Who's there?

Howl.

Howl who?

That dog is howling because he's excited to see you!

Knock knock,

Who's there?

Hide.

Hide who?

Come find me. I am hiding from you.

Knock knock,

Who's there?

Later.

Later who?

I have to go, but we can hang out later.

Knock knock,

Who's there?

Early.

Early who?

The early bird gets the worm.

Knock knock,

Who's there?

Guess.

Guess who?

Can you guess who it is at your door?

Knock knock,

Who's there?

Suzy.

Suzy who?

Suzy is over there, and she wants to talk to you.

Knock knock,

Who's there?

Two.

Two who?

Two can play that game.

Knock knock,

Who's there?

Who.

Who who?

Oh wow, that's a great owl impression!

Knock knock,

Who's there?

Catch.

Catch who?

You've got to catch up. I am way ahead of you.

Knock knock,

Who's there?

Close.

Close who?

Can we close the door? It's so cold.

Knock knock,

Who's there?

Lying.

Lying who?

You've been lying down all day. Get up and let's go play.

Knock knock,

Who's there?

Jump.

Jump who?

The cow jumped over the moon!

Knock knock,

Who's there?

When.

When who?

When are we going to stop all this knocking?

Knock knock,

Who's there?

Coffee.

Coffee who?

Would you like some coffee and tea with me?

Knock knock,

Who's there?

Burgers.

Burgers who?

Would you like burgers for lunch?

Knock knock,

Who's there?

Corn.

Corn who?

Unicorn!!

Knock knock,

Who's there?

Rainbow.

Rainbow who?

There is a rainbow unicorn flying above you.

Knock knock,

Who's there?

Banana.

Banana who?

Banana split!

Knock knock,

Who's there?

Can.

Can who?

Can these knock knock jokes get any funnier?

Knock knock,

Who's there?

Time.

Time who?

Time for another knock knock joke.

Knock knock,

Who's there?

Let's go.

Let's go who?

Let's all go to the movies.

Knock knock,

Who's there?

Dark.

Dark who?

It's too dark outside. I'm scared.

Knock knock,

Who's there?

Wrap.

Wrap who?

You need to wrap yourself up. It's cold outside today.

Knock knock,

Who's there?

Can you.

Can you who?

Can you come out and play with me?

Knock knock,

Who's there?

Camping.

Camping who?

We're all going camping!

Knock knock,

Who's there?

Ice.

Ice who?

Ice cubes for your drink.

Knock knock,

Who's there?

Trees.

Trees who?

The trees stay green until fall!

Knock knock,

Who's there?

About.

About who?

Is it about time for dinner?

Knock knock,

Who's there?

About.

About who?

About time to eat lunch isn't it mom?

Knock knock,

Who's there?

Good.

Good who?

If I'm good, can I have some candy?

Knock knock,

Who's there?

Mama.

Mama who?

Mama, I sure do love you.

Knock knock,

Who's there?

Fly.

Fly who?

Oh no, I found a fly in my soup.

Knock knock,

Who's there?

Uh oh.

Uh oh who?

Uh oh, I ate way more than I should have.

Knock knock,

Who's there?

Have.

Have who?

Have another piece of pie dear.

Knock knock,

Who's there?

Are.

Are who?

Are there any more cookies for me and you?

Knock knock,

Who's there?

Barbeque.

Barbeque who?

We have barbeque ribs waiting for you.

Knock knock,

Who's there?

Been.

Been who?

It's been a while since we have seen you.

Knock knock,

Who's there?

Bees.

Bees who?

Bees sure are good at making honey, aren't they?

Knock knock,

Who's there?

Burnt.

Burnt who?

It looks like we burn the toast. We better try it again.

Knock knock,

Who's there?

Butter.

Butter who?

Can you butter this toast for me, please?

Knock knock,

Who's there?

Horse.

Horse who?

We gotta stop horsing around here.

Knock knock,

Who's there?

Horse.

Horse who?

Horse sense!

Knock knock,

Who's there?

Horse.

Horse who?

The horse ate all of his hay. Now he's nice and full.

Knock knock,

Who's there?

Delicious.

Delicious who?

Delicious apples are the best.

Knock knock,

Who's there?

Broccoli.

Broccoli who?

Finish your broccoli, then you can have dessert.

Knock knock,

Who's there?

Ham.

Ham who?

I'd like ham and eggs for breakfast, please.

Knock knock,

Who's there?

Pizza.

Pizza who?

Can you hand me a slice of that pizza, please?

Knock knock,

Who's there?

Don't.

Don't who?

Don't eat that apple. There's a worm in it.

Knock knock,

Who's there?

Sing.

Sing who?

The reason I sing so loudly is so that you and everyone can hear me.

Knock knock,

Who's there?

Cheese.

Cheese who?

Nacho cheese!

Knock knock,

Who's there?

Mom.

Mom who?

It's your mother.

Knock knock,

Who's there?

Chip.

Chip who?

Chocolate chip cookies.

Knock knock,

Who's there?

Chip.

Chip who?

Chip off the old block.

Knock knock,

Who's there?

Past.

Past who?

It's past your bedtime. Go to sleep love.

Knock knock,

Who's there?

Honey.

Honey who?

Honey is good for you!

Knock knock,

Who's there?

Nephew.

Nephew who?

It's your nephew silly open up!

Knock knock,

Who's there?

Niece.

Niece who?

It's your niece, and I can't reach the doorbell. I am too small.

Knock knock,

Who's there?

Blood.

Blood who?

Blood is thicker than water.

Knock knock,

Who's there?

Stranger.

Stranger who?

I'm sorry my mother told me not to answer the door for strangers.

Knock knock,

Who's there?

Hard.

Hard who?

It's hard to hear you, please speak up so I can.

Knock knock,

Who's there?

Best friend.

Best friend who?

It's your best friend, and you don't know me?

Knock knock,

Who's there?

Opportunity.

Opportunity who?

Opportunity doesn't knock I thought?

Knock knock,

Who's there?

Beat.

Beat who?

The beat goes on.

Knock knock,

Who's there?

Leave.

Leave who?

Leave me alone.

Knock knock,

Who's there?

Police.

Police who?

We're asking the questions here ma'am.

Knock knock,

Who's there?

Can.

Can who?

Can you feel the love tonight?

Knock knock,

Who's there?

Gum.

Gum who?

Why did you take my gum?

Knock knock,

Who's there?

Pasta.

Pasta who?

We're having pasta for dinner.

Knock knock,

Who's there?

Peanut.

Peanut who?

Would you like a peanut or a cashew?

Knock knock,

Who's there?

Pick.

Pick who?

Pick on someone your own size.

Knock knock,

Who's there?

Shoe.

Shoe who?

You're not a shoe. They go on your feet.

Knock knock,

Who's there?

Fish.

Fish who?

Fish and chips, please.

Knock knock,

Who's there?

Pudding.

Pudding who?

Pudding face!

Knock knock,

Who's there?

Sit.

Sit who?

Sit down please it's time to eat.

Knock knock,

Who's there?

Turkey.

Turkey who?

Turkey's go gobble gobble!

Knock knock,

Who's there?

Turn.

Turn who?

Can you turn down the volume please it's too loud here?

Knock knock,

Who's there?

Up.

Up who?

Turn up the radio; it's too quiet in here.

Knock knock,

Who's there?

Chocolate.

Chocolate who?

Did you save me any of the chocolate cake?

Knock knock,

Who's there?

Father.

Father who?

Your father is here.

Knock knock,

Who's there?

Love.

Love who?

I will always love you.

Knock knock,

Who's there?

Me.

Me who?

You forgot who I am already?

Knock knock,

Who's there?

One.

One who?

One for the money, two for the show, three to get ready and four to go!!

Knock knock,

Who's there?

Clear.

Clear who?

Clear the way please I need to get in.

Knock knock,

Who's there?

Pirate.

Pirate who?

A pirate says argggg!

Knock knock,

Who's there?

Real.

Real who?

Real pleasure to meet you.

Knock knock,

Who's there?

Walk.

Walk who?

I'd walk a thousand miles for you.

Knock knock,

Who's there?

Want to?

Want to who?

Want to hang out with me right now?

Knock knock,

Who's there?

Chicken.

Chicken who?

Chickens go bawk bawk!

Knock knock,

Who's there?

Foot.

Foot who?

My foot is caught in your door.

Knock knock,

Who's there?

Key.

Key who?

My key doesn't fit.

Knock knock,

Who's there?

Lock.

Lock who?

You'll lock the door after we leave, won't you?

Knock knock,

Who's there?

Sure.

Sure who?

You sure shut your door loud.

Knock knock,

Who's there?

Doorbell.

Doorbell who?

Does your doorbell work, or should I knock again?

Knock knock,

Who's there?

Nice.

Nice who?

Nice to meet you.

Knock knock,

Who's there?

Pretty.

Pretty who?

Pretty house you have here.

Knock knock,

Who's there?

Goodness.

Goodness who?

Goodness I think I have the wrong house.

Knock knock,

Who's there?

Anybody.

Anybody who?

Doesn't anybody want to let me in?

Knock knock,

Who's there?

Money.

Money who?

Can I have some money for the movies tonight?

Knock knock,

Who's there?

Before.

Before who?

I think we've knocked on this door before.

Knock knock,

Who's there?

To.

To who?

No, no the expression is to whom.

Knock knock,

Who's there?

Cars.

Cars who?

Cars go beep beep beep!

Knock knock,

Who's there?

Nap.

Nap who?

You look tired do you need a nap?

Knock knock,

Who's there?

Lost.

Lost who?

If you're lost, I can lend you a map?

Knock knock

Who's there?

Sing.

Sing who?

I sang so loudly grandma could hear me.

Knock knock,

Who's there?

Doorbell.

Doorbell who?

Your doorbell works now, so we don't have to knock.

Knock knock,

Who's there?

Ask.

Ask who?

I will ask the questions.

Knock knock,

Who's there?

Pigs.

Pigs who?

Pigs go oink oink!!

Knock knock,

Who's there?

Can you?

Can you who?

Can you help me with my schoolwork, please?

Knock knock,

Who's there?

Question.

Question who?

I have a question for you, but if you're busy, I can ask later.

Knock knock,

Who's there?

Which way?

Which way who?

Which way is the way home?

Knock knock,

Who's there?

Lost.

Lost who?

I'm lost do you have a compass?

Knock knock,

Who's there?

Mosquito.

Mosquito who?

A mosquito just bit me.

Knock knock,

Who's there?

The door.

The door who?

The door was closed, so I knocked.

Knock knock,

Who's there?

Lean.

Lean who?

I think I leaned too hard on your door.

Knock knock,

Who's there?

Pants.

Pants who?

Your pants are going to fall. You're not wearing a belt.

Knock knock,

Who's there?

Letter.

Letter who?

I sent a letter saying I was coming.

Knock knock,

Who's there?

Love.

Love who?

I love you, and I want everyone to know it.

Knock knock,

Who's there?

Vampire.

Vampire who?

Be a vampire this Halloween!

Knock knock,

Who's there?

Penny waterbottom.

Penny waterbottom who?

How many waterbottoms do you know?

Knock knock,

Who's there?

How.

How who?

Well, I am just fine today. Thank you so much, how are you?

Knock knock,

Who's there?

Sweet and sour.

Sweet and sour who?

Sweet and sour chicken.

Knock knock,

Who's there?

Sad.

Sad who?

I am sad that you never recognize me.

Knock knock,

Who's there?

Yarn.

Yarn who?

Do you like the sweater I made you?

Knock knock,

Who is there?

No.

No who?

There's no point in pretending you don't know who I am.

Knock knock,

Who's there?

Bother.

Bother who?

Is all this knock knocking bothering you?

Knock knock,

Who's there?

Lost key.

Lost key who?

I lost my key, and I need you to let me in.

Knock knock,

Who's there?

Will you.

Will you who?

Will you be mine forever?

Knock knock,

Who's there?

Ought.

Ought who?

You ought to be able to recognize your own father.

Knock knock,

Who's there?

Dance.

Dance who?

Dance with me.

Knock knock,

Who's there?

Pizza.

Pizza who?

Is there any pizza left? I am hungry.

Knock knock,

Who's there?

Bored.

Bored who?

I am bored. We should do something fun.

Knock knock,

Who's there?

Poem.

Poem who?

I wrote you a poem.

Knock knock,

Who's there?

Barbeque.

Barbeque who?

Let's have a barbeque!!!

Knock knock,

Who's there?

Bee.

Bee who?

Bee ware on Halloween!

Knock knock,

Who's there?

How.

How who?

How are you dressing this Halloween?

Knock knock,

Who's there?

Better.

Better who?

I better not tell you. It might be too scary!

Knock knock,

Kiss.

Kiss who?

Please kiss me, my wonderful prince!

Knock knock,

Who's there?

Clear.

Clear who?

You need to clear the hallway for your package.

Knock knock,

Who's there?

Ice cream.

Ice cream who?

Ice cream is amazing on a hot day.

Knock knock,

Who's there?

Will you.

Will you who?

Will you be my valentine?

Knock knock,

Who's there?

Fix.

Fix who?

Your gonna have to fix your doorbell. It's broken again.

Knock knock,

Who's there?

Keen.

Keen who?

I am so keen on you!

Knock knock,

Who's there?

Smitten.

Smitten who?

I am smitten with you!

Knock knock,

Who's there?

Hand.

Hand who?

My hand is hurting from all this knocking.

Knock knock,

Who's there?

Girl scouts.

Girl scouts who?

Let's get some girl scout cookies.

Knock knock,

Who's there?

Must.

Must who?

Must you be so nosy?

Knock knock,

Who's there?

Know.

Know who?

We know all the knock knock jokes there are!

Knock knock,

Who's there?

Wrap.

Wrap who?

You have to wrap it up carefully. It's fragile!

Knock knock,

Who's there?

Wanna.

Wanna who?

I wanna hold your hand.

Knock knock,

Who's there?

Two.

Two who?

Two is company, but three is a crowd.

Knock knock,

Own.

Own who?

I own a new car. Would you like a ride?

Knock knock,

Who's there?

You can.

You can who?

You can say that joke again!

Knock knock,

Who's there?

Nice.

Nice who?

I am a real nice guy, just like you.

Knock knock,

Who's there?

Sick.

Sick who?

I'm getting sick of all this cold weather.

Knock knock,

Who's there?

Vacation.

Vacation who?

For vacation, let's go to Miami!

Knock knock,

Who's there?

Early.

Early who?

Early to bed, early to rise.

Knock knock,

Who's there?

Suzy.

Suzy who?

Suzy left. Now we have to make all of the pies.

Knock knock,

Who's there?

Fish.

Fish who?

We're going to have fish and chips today.

Knock knock,

Who's there?

Lend.

Lend who?

Can you please lend me some money?

Knock knock,

Who's there?

Super.

Super who?

Superheroes!!

Knock knock,

Who's there?

Rustle.

Rustle who?

Let's rustle up some good food!

Knock knock,

Football.

Football who?

Does anyone in this town play football?

Knock knock,

Who's there?

Pick.

Pick who?

Would you like to pick the game we play today?

Knock knock,

Who's there?

Ballgame.

Ballgame who?

Take me out to the ballgame, please!

Knock knock,

Who's there?

Aunt.

Aunt who?

Knock knock,

Who's there?

Aunt

Aunt who?

Knock knock,

Aunt

Aunt who?

Knock knock,

Who's there?

Uncle.

Uncle who?

Bet you're glad I said uncle instead of aunt this time, right?

Knock knock,

Who's there?

Any.

Any who?

Is anybody home today?

Knock knock,

Who's there?

Wanna.

Wanna who?

Wanna know what you're getting for Christmas?

Knock knock,

Who's there?

Deck.

Deck who?

Deck the halls with bells and holly!

Knock knock,

Who's there?

Turkey.

Turkey who?

Has anyone seen the Thanksgiving turkey?

Knock knock,

Who's there?

No.

No who?

Nobody, April fools! I tricked you!

Knock knock,

Who's there?

New year.

New year who?

Have a happy new year!

Knock knock,

Who's there?

Santa.

Santa who?

Santa brought a bunch of presents for you.

Knock knock,

Who's there?

Call.

Call who?

Call me if you hear Santa, please?

Knock knock,

Who's there?

Coal.

Coal who?

I'm so glad I didn't get coal this Christmas!

Knock knock,

Who's there?

Nickle.

Nickle who?

A nickel used to be worth a lot more money.

Knock knock,

Who's there?

Blood.

Blood who?

I want to suck your blood!

Knock knock,

Who's there?

Who?

Who who?

Who is that monster over there?

Knock knock,

Who's there?

Gargle.

Gargle who?

If your throat is still sore, then you should gargle for it.

Knock knock,

Who's there?

Who.

Who who?

Who did you think I was a ghost?

Knock knock,

Who's there?

Please.

Please who?

Please give me some candy.

Knock knock,

Who's there?

Normally.

Normally who?

Normally on Halloween, I say trick or treat!

Knock knock,

Who's there?

Cow.

Cow who?

Can a cow really jump over the moon?

Knock knock,

Who's there?

Tie.

Tie who?

Knock knock,

Who's there?

Borrow.

Borrow who?

Can I borrow a marker from you?

Knock, knock,

Who's there?

Howard.

Howard who?

Well if you don't know Howard, what makes you think I do?

Knock knock,

Who's there?

Tickle.

Tickle who?

I'm going to tickle you!

Knock knock,

Who's there?

Forgot.

Forgot who?

I'm sorry I am confused. Do I know you?

Knock knock,

Who's there?

Stuck.

Stuck who?

The door is stuck, we can't get in.

Knock knock,

Who's there?

Police.

Police who?

Police now open up its cold outside.

Knock knock,

Who's there?

Can't.

Can't who?

You can't ask, it's a secret.

Knock knock,

Who's there?

Remember.

Remember who?

I don't remember.

Knock knock,

Who's there?

Tissue.

Tissue who?

A tissue is great for blowing your nose when it's runny.

Knock knock,

Who's there,

A broken pencil,

A broken pencil who?

Never mind this joke lost its point.

Knock knock,

Who's there?

Stay.

Stay who?

Stay home from school if your sick today.

Knock knock

Who's there?

Me.

Me who?

You said you would remember me.

Knock knock,

Who's there?

Birthday.

Birthday who?

Birthday greetings from me to you!

Knock knock,

Who's there?

Adore.

Adore who?

Adorable us wishing you a happy birthday!

Knock knock,

Who's there?

Come.

Come who?

Oh come all ye faithful.

Knock knock,

Who's there?

Holly.

Holly who?

Have a holly jolly Christmas to you!

Knock knock,

Who's there?

Which one?

Which one who?

Which one of you wants some birthday cake?

Knock knock,

Who's there?

What?

What who?

What are you doing?

Knock knock,

Who's there?

Honey.

Honey who?

Honey, do you love me?

Knock knock,

Who's there?

Eat.

Eat who?

Be sure to finish eating your fruit.

Knock knock,

Who's there?

Park.

Park who?

Let's all go to the park!

Knock knock,

Who's there?

Canine.

Canine who?

Our canine needs to go to the vet.

Knock knock,

Who's there?

Right.

Right who?

Right you are young man.

Knock, knock,

Who's there?

Sore.

Sore who?

I have a sore wrist today.

Knock knock,

Who's there?

Right.

Right who?

Your right on time today.

Knock knock,

Who's there?

Television.

Television who?

What's on the television tonight?

Knock knock,

Who's there?

Yee.

Yee who?

Yee haw I'm a cowboy!

Knock knock,

Who's there?

Why?

Why who?

Why are you always asking who?

Knock knock,

Who's there?

Need.

Need who?

I need you to help me, please.

Knock knock,

Who's there?

Behave.

Behave who?

Behave, or you're going to get yourself into trouble.

Knock knock,

Who's there?

Any.

Any who?

Anybody that wants to see you.

Knock knock,

Who's there?

Friends.

Friends who?

All your friends came to play with you.

Knock knock,

Who's there?

Door.

Door who?

There's a door between us. I can't see you.

Knock knock,

Who's there?

Fried.

Fried who?

Would you like some fried chicken? I saved some for you.

Knock knock,

Who's there?

Father.

Father who?

Like father like son.

Knock knock,

Who's there?

Chimp.

Chimp who?

Chimpanzees at the zoo!

Knock knock,

Who's there?

Know.

Know who?

You know me silly. Let me in the door.

Knock knock,

Who's there?

Comb.

Comb who?

Sweetie comb your hair before you go to school.

Knock knock,

Who's there?

I think.

I think who?

I think I wanna marry you!

Knock knock,

Who's there?

I do too.

I do too who?

I think I wanna marry you too!

Knock knock,

Who's there?

Instead.

Instead who?

Instead of letting me in, you're making me stand in the rain.

Knock knock,

Who's there?

Me.

Me who?

You should know my name were best friends.

Knock knock,

Who's there?

Nana.

Nana who?

Don't you sass your nana now.

Knock knock,

Who's there?

Honey.

Honey who?

Honey, I am home.

Knock knock,

Who's there?

Sweets.

Sweets who?

I ate too many sweets. Now my stomach hurts.

Knock knock,

Who's there?

Betcha.

Betcha who?

Betcha can't guess who's at your door.

Knock knock,

Who's there?

I'll go.

I'll go who?

I'll go anywhere with you that you want me to.

Knock knock,

Who's there?

Hula.

Hula who?

Oh yes! I'd love to hula hoop with you!

Knock knock,

Who's there?

Would.

Would who?

Would you do me a favor and open the door, please.

Knock knock,

Who's there?

To be.

To be who?

To be or not to be, that is the question, right?

Knock knock,

Who's there?

Tune.

Tune who?

If you tune a piano, it sounds better.

Knock knock,

Who's there?

Pain.

Pain who?

It's a pain to have to keep knocking on the door.

Knock knock,

Who's there?

Duck.

Duck who?

Ducks say quack quack quack not who.

Knock knock,

Who's there?

Hello.

Hello who?

Hello kitty cat it's nice to see you.

Knock knock,

Who's there?

Far.

Far who?

So far so good.

Knock knock,

Who's there?

Go for.

Go for who?

I could go for a cup of hot cocoa right now. How about you?

Knock knock,

Who's there?

Crack.

Crack who?

When are you going to stop cracking this bad knock knock jokes?

Knock knock,

Who's there?

Chickens.

Chickens who?

Don't count your chickens before they have hatched.

Knock knock,

Who's there?

Bee.

Bee who?

It looks like a bee stung me on the arm.

Knock knock,

Who's there?

Lost.

Lost who?

I got lost on the way to see you.

Knock knock,

Who's there?

Thank you.

Thank you who?

Thank you for inviting me into your home.

Knock knock,

Who's there?

Today.

Today who?

Today is the first day of the rest of your life.

Knock knock,

Who's there?

Easter.

Easter who?

Are there any more Easter eggs to decorate?

Knock knock,

Who's there?

Do you want to?

Do you want to who?

Do you want to decorate Easter eggs with me?

Knock knock,

Who's there?

Would you like one?

Would you like one who?

Would you like one of the chocolate bunnies?

Knock knock,

Who's there?

When.

When who?

When is the Easter bunny coming? I want to see him!!!

Knock knock,

Who's there?

Spaghetti.

Spaghetti who?

Spaghetti and meatballs are the best!

Knock knock,

Who's there?

Boo.

Boo who?

Ghosts don't say who they say boo!

Knock knock,

Who's there?

Patrick.

Patrick who?

I wish you a happy Saint Patrick's Day!

Knock knock,

Who's there?

Close.

Close who?

Close but not quite.

Knock knock,

Who's there?

Peas.

Peas who?

Were two peas in a pod.

Knock knock,

Who's there?

Shoes.

Shoes who?

You're not a shoe silly you're a person.

Knock knock,

Who's there?

Break.

Break who?

If you're tired, you can rest and take a break.

Knock knock,

Who's there?

Clothes.

Clothes who?

Be careful not to rip your clothes.

Knock knock,

Who's there?

Car horn.

Car horn who?

Car horns go honk honk!

Knock knock,

Who's there?

Neighbors.

Neighbors who?

The neighbors are singing so loud.

Knock knock,

Who's there?

E.T.

E.T. who?

How many aliens named E.T. do you know?

Knock knock,

Who's there?

Can.

Can who?

Can this door open or are we sleeping outside?

Knock knock,

Who's there?

Water.

Water who?

Will you water the plants, please?

Knock knock,

Who's there?

The key.

The key who?

You gave me the wrong key to your door.

Knock knock,

Who's there?

Déjà vu.

Déjà vu who?

Knock knock,

Who's there?

I can't remember.

Knock knock,

Who's there?

Need.

Need who?

I need a little money. My rent is due.

Knock knock,

Who's there?

Purse.

Purse who?

Don't you know? I control the purse strings here.

Knock knock,

Who's there?

Lend.

Lend who?

I will lend you money if you promise to pay me back.

Knock knock,

Who's there?

Package.

Package who?

I need you to open the door because I have a package for you.

Knock knock,

Who's there?

Dragging.

Dragging who?

We gotta stop dragging our feet and get to work.

Knock knock,

Who's there?

Knee.

Knee who?

My knee always hurts when its cold out.

Knock knock,

Who's there?

I will be

I will be who?

I will be a seahorses uncle.

Knock knock,

Who's there?

Music.

Music who?

I think I'll just listen to music today.

Knock knock,

Who's there?

Demand.

Demand who?

I demand a hug and kiss from you.

Knock knock,

Who's there?

Email.

Email who?

Email me later if you can.

Knock knock,

Who's there?

Apple.

Apple who?

An apple a day keeps the doctor away.

Knock knock,

Who's there?

An.

An who?

An eye for an eye, a tooth for a tooth.

Knock knock,

Who's there?

Are we?

Are we who?

Are we on the same page here?

Knock knock,

Who's there?

Bowling,

Bowling who?

Are you coming bowling with us?

Knock knock,

Who's there?

I need.

I need who?

I need to go to the bathroom.

Knock knock,

Who's there?

Every.

Every who?

Every time I come over, we do this.

Knock knock,

Who's there?

Every.

Every who?

Every cloud has a silver lining.

Knock knock,

Who's there?

Bury.

Bury who?

Bury the treasure so that no one will find it.

Knock knock,

Who's there?

Been.

Been who?

I've been away for a while, but I sure did miss you.

Knock knock,

Who's there?

Carry.

Carry who?

Don't you think you're getting a little carried away, honey?

Knock knock,

Who's there?

Car.

Car who?

Sweetie, cars don't belong in school.

Knock knock,

Who's there?

Shampoo.

Shampoo who?

We gotta wash your hair, honey.

Knock knock,

Who's there?

Check.

Check who?

We're here to check the plumbing for you today.

Knock knock,

Who's there?

Clean.

Clean who?

Clean up your room please. It's a mess.

Knock knock,

Who's there?

Since you been.

Since you been who?

Since you've been gone, I have really missed you.

Knock knock,

Who's there?

Dog.

Dog who?

A dog is man's best friend.

Knock knock,

Who's there?

Meal.

Meal who?

That meal was fit for a king.

Knock knock,

Who's there?

Cracking,

Cracking who?

Cracking me up you are!

Knock knock,

Who's there?

Errand.

Errand who?

I have a few errands to run, but I will be back later.

Knock knock,

Who's there?

Exhausted.

Exhausted who?

I'm so exhausted. May I please come inside?

Knock knock,

Who's there?

Afraid.

Afraid who?

Who's afraid of the big bad wolf?

Knock knock,

Who's there?

Generally.

Generally who?

Generally, I do not tell such amazing knock knock jokes.

Knock knock,

Who's there?

When.

When who?

When are we going to hang out again?

Knock knock,

Who's there?

How many.

How many who?

How many times should I repeat myself to you?

Knock knock,

Who's there?

Hair.

Hair who?

My hair is falling out from my head.

Knock knock,

Who's there?

Hot.

Hot who?

It's far too hot in here today.

Knock knock,

Who's there?

Hello.

Hello who?

My name is Katarina, not who.

Knock knock,

Who's there?

All.

All who?

It's not all lost. We all have each other and family.

Knock knock,

Who's there?

Driving.

Driving who?

What are you driving at here?

Knock knock,

Who's there?

Later.

Later who?

I don't think Ben is here. I will see him later.

Knock knock,

Who's there?

This way.

This way who?

I am going this way. You go that way.

Knock knock,

Who's there?

Clue.

Clue who?

I have no clue what's going on here.

Knock knock,

Who's there?

Pickle.

Pickle who?

I want a pickle. Can you get me one?

Knock knock,

Who's there?

I knew.

I knew who?

I knew it was you here.

Knock knock,

Who's there?

Bike.

Bike who?

Come bike with me. It's so sunny today.

Knock knock,

Who's there?

Eggs.

Eggs who?

Your eggs are done love, come eat.

Knock knock,

Who's there?

Where.

Where who?

Where are we?

Knock knock,

Who's there?

Joined.

Joined who?

Don't you know we're joined at the hip?

Knock knock,

Who's there?

Open.

Open who?

Your door was open, but I knocked to be polite.

Knock knock,

Who's there?

Time.

Time who?

Just in time for dinner guys.

Knock knock,

Who's there?

Cell.

Cell who?

Just in case you want it, here's my cell number.

Knock knock,

Who's there?

Lonely.

Lonely who?

I'm so lonely out here alone.

Knock knock,

Who's there?

Lean.

Lean who?

If you lean in. I will tell you a secret.

Knock knock,

Who's there?

Let's go.

Let's go who?

Let's go now before we're late.

Knock knock,

Who's there?

Look.

Look who?

Look before you leap.

Knock knock,

Who's there?

Look.

Look who?

Look out. Here comes another joke.

Knock knock,

Who's there?

Make.

Make who?

Make up your mind.

Knock knock,

Who's there?

Money.

Money who?

Money doesn't grow on trees guys.

Knock knock,

Who's there?

Nod.

Nod who?

Just nod your head if you get what I am saying.

Knock knock,

Who's there?

Who.

Who who?

Who let the owl out of the tree?

Knock knock,

Who's there?

Pull.

Pull who?

Pull up a chair, and we'll talk.

Knock knock,

Who's there?

Falling.

Falling who?

I think I am falling in love with you.

Knock knock,

Who's there?

Fill.

Fill who?

Fill up my gas tank; I'm running super low.

Knock knock,

Who's there?

Clean.

Clean who?

Clean as a whistle.

Knock knock,

Who's there?

Roll.

Roll who?

Roll with the punches.

Knock knock,

Who's there?

Rain.

Rain who?

Watch out, it's raining cats and dogs out here.

Knock knock,

Who's there?

Ring.

Ring who?

Why are you ringing the bell? It doesn't do any good.

Knock knock,

Who's there?

Sat.

Sat who?

I accidentally sat on my phone. I'm sorry I couldn't call you.

Knock knock,

Who's there?

Run.

Run who?

Let's run a marathon!

Knock knock,

Who's there?

Ring.

Ring who?

Ring around the roses, ring around the roses.

Knock knock,

Who's there?

Read.

Read who?

Read a little more and find out.

Knock knock,

Who's there?

Read.

Read who?

Read a book. It's good for you.

Knock knock,

Who's there?

Roof.

Roof who?

The roof is leaking; we need to fix it.

Knock knock,

Who's there?

Same.

Same who?

The same person who knocked the last time.

Knock knock,

Who's there?

Doctor.

Doctor who?

Is there a doctor in the house?

Knock knock,

Who's there?

Laughing.

Laughing who?

You're not laughing at these knock knock jokes, are you?

Knock knock,

Who's there?

You need to feed.

You need to feed who?

You need to feed the cat before dinner, will you?

Knock knock,

Who's there?

Someday.

Someday who?

Someday my prince will come.

Knock knock,

Who's there?

Where.

Where who?

Where did I put my car keys? Do you know?

Knock knock,

Who's there?

When.

When who?

When was the last time you did your homework?

Knock knock,

Who's there?

You need to lock.

You need to lock who?

Remember you always need to lock your door.

Knock knock,

Who's there?

Wanda Sue.

Wanda Sue who?

Wanda Sue from across the street.

Knock knock,

Who's there?

See.

See who?

Can't you see I'm head over heels for you?

Knock knock,

Who's there?

Rain.

Rain who?

Raindrops are falling on my mane and getting it wet.

Knock knock,

Who's there?

Miss.

Miss who?

Do you miss your unicorn because she misses you?

Knock knock,

Who's there?

Sparkles.

Sparkles who?

Sparks the unicorn is sparkling for you.

Knock knock,

Who's there?

Boo.

Boo who?

Oh sweetheart unicorns aren't scary. Don't be frightened.

Knock knock,

Who's there?

Karate.

Karate who?

Unicorn karate chop!

Knock knock,

Who's there?

Wanna.

Wanna who?

Wanna play hide and seek? My sparkly horn makes me easy to find.

Knock knock,

Who's there?

Rainbow.

Rainbow who?

Rainbow horn of the unicorn!

Knock knock,

Who's there?

Ho ho.

Ho ho who?

Ho ho ho is Santa. He and I are best friends.

Knock knock,

Who's there?

Door.

Door who?

The door is too small for a unicorn to fit through.

Knock knock,

Who's there?

Chocolate.

Chocolate who?

Of course, unicorns love chocolate!

Knock knock,

Who's there?

Untied.

Untied who?

Your shoelaces are untied.

Knock knock,

Who's there?

First.

First who?

Today is the first day of flying season for unicorns.

Knock knock,

Who's there?

Play.

Play who?

Would you like to play with us unicorns today?

Knock knock,

Who's there?

Unicorn.

Unicorn who?

How many unicorns do you know silly?

Knock knock,

Who's there?

Remember.

Remember who?

Remember your unicorn friend!

Knock knock,

Who's there?

Crown.

Crown who?

My mane makes a rainbow crown around my head.

Knock knock,

Who's there?

Unicorn.

Unicorn who?

Unicorns sparkle like pretty diamonds.

Knock knock,

Who's there,

Bite.

Bite who?

Don't worry I won't bite you. You're not what unicorns eat.

Knock knock,

Who's there?

Favorite.

Favorite who?

A unicorn's favorite food is rainbow nuggets!

Knock knock,

Who's there?

Favorite too.

Favorite too who?

A unicorn's other favorite food is unicorn bites.

Knock knock,

Who's there?

Outside.

Outside who?

We were all outside looking for you.

Knock knock,

Who's there?

Heard.

Heard who?

The unicorns heard you were home and came to visit you!

Knock knock,

Who's there?

I can.

I can who?

I bet I can tell more unicorn knock knock jokes than you.

Knock knock,

Who's there?

Please.

Please who?

Will you come and play with me and my unicorn friends, please?

Knock knock,

Who's there?

Merry.

Merry who?

Merry Christmas from all of us unicorns to you!

Knock knock,

Who's there?

Holly.

Holly who?

Holly jolly holidays from our unicorns to you.

Knock knock,

Who's there?

How.

How who?

You must know it's your special rainbow friend knocking.

Knock knock,

Who's there?

I.

I who?

Your unicorn friend is here.

Knock knock,

Who's there?

You.

You who?

You are here to play with us unicorns in the clouds.

Knock knock,

Who's there?

Be.

Be who?

Be your amazing unicorn sparkly self.

Knock knock,

Who's there?

You.

You who?

My special unicorn eyes see you!

Knock knock,

Who's there?

Me.

Me who?

You see me with your extra special eyes!

Knock knock,

Who's there?

Owl.

Owl who?

Did you know the owls fly alongside the unicorns too?

Knock knock,

Who's there?

I.

I who?

I love you! My special unicorn.

Knock knock,

Who's there?

Moo.

Moo who?

Unicorns don't say moo.

Knock knock,

Who's there?

Atch.

Atch who?

Ugh oh when a unicorn sneezes, glitter sprays everywhere. I'll need a big tissue!

Knock knock,

Who's there?

Pee.

Pee who?

Peekaboo! My special eyes have landed on you!

Knock knock,

Who's there?

Beat.

Beat who?

Let's listen to a great beat as we fly high in the sky.

Knock knock,

Who's there?

Adore.

Adore who?

Unicorns all adore you!

Knock knock,

Who's there?

Bee.

Bee who?

The honeybees can fly with us too.

Knock knock,

Who's there?

Business.

Business who?

Unicorn official business.

Knock knock,

Who's there?

Remember.

Remember who?

Remember all the unicorns are unique, just like you.

Knock knock,

Who's there?

Thank you.

Thank you who?

Thank you for letting us make magical memories with you.

Knock knock,

Who's there?

Ready.

Ready who?

Ready set run!!

Knock knock,

Who's there?

Better.

Better who?

I hope the purple unicorn feels better soon.

Knock knock,

Who's there?

Alphabet.

Alphabet who?

Alphabet soup. Us unicorns are great spellers.

Knock knock,

Who's there?

How.

How who?

How are you I heard one of the unicorns is blue?

Knock knock,

Who's there?

Glitter.

Glitter who?

Unicorns are famous for being glittery too!

Knock knock,
Who's there?
Me.
Me who?
I'm standing right in front of you with a rainbow tail. Surely you can't miss me, right?

Knock knock,
Who's there?
Alias.
Alias who?
I am sorry I don't think that the unicorns know you?

Knock knock,
Who's there?
Boo.
Boo who?
Oh sweetheart don't be scared. Unicorns are super friendly.

Knock knock,
Who's there?
Stuck.
Stuck who?
Your door is stuck, and I can't fit my hooves inside.

Knock knock,

Who's there?

Love.

Love who?

Do you love your rainbow friend? We all love you.

Knock knock,

Who's there?

Cashew.

Cashew who?

Do you like cashews? This unicorn likes peanuts.

Knock knock,

Who's there?

Pen.

Pen who?

I don't need a pen. Unicorns can't write.

Knock knock,

Who's there?

Come on.

Come on who?

Come on and play with us. We're playing rainbow speed races!

Knock knock,

Who's there?

Who.

Who who?

I'm sorry unicorns can't speak owl.

Knock knock,

Who's there?

Forget.

Forget who?

Forget no one. Remember all of the unicorn friends of yours.

Knock knock,

Who's there?

Remember.

Remember who?

Remember playing unicorn games with me.

Knock knock,

Who's there?

Sure.

Sure who?

Us magical beings sure do love you.

Knock knock,

Who's there?

Don't.

Don't who?

Don't you want to invite us in? Us unicorns get cold easily.

Knock knock,

Who's there?

Where.

Where who?

Where did you go? I've got four unicorns looking for you!

Knock knock,

Who's there?

Don't.

Don't who?

I don't want to go to unicorn school without you.

Knock knock,

Who's there?

Please.

Please who?

Please join us for unicorn games, it will be no fun without you.

Knock knock,

Who's there?

Whatcha.

Whatcha who?

Whatcha doing today? Are you going to come braid unicorn hair?

Knock knock,

Who's there?

In time.

In time who?

You made it just in time for unicorn cake!

Knock knock,

Who's there?

How.

How who?

How are sure it's not another unicorn knocking?

Knock knock,

Who's there?

Unicorn school.

Unicorn school who?

Don't you remember, we have unicorn school today?

Knock knock,

Who's there?

Halloween candy.

Halloween candy who?

I think us unicorns ate all the Halloween candy without you.

Knock knock,

Who's there?

Treat.

Treat who?

I get unicorn treats this Halloween!

Knock knock,

Who's there?

Wrong.

Wrong who?

I think this unicorn has the wrong door.

Knock knock,

Who's there?

Presents.

Presents who?

Open up. Us unicorns have magical presents for you today!

Knock knock,

Who's there?

Crystal unicorn.

Crystal unicorn who?

Did you know my crystal unicorn eyes see you!

Knock knock,

Who's there?

Let.

Let who?

Let me in so we can play glitter races!

Knock knock,

Who's there?

I win.

I win who?

I won the glitter races so unfortunately, you lose.

Knock knock,

Who's there?

Dino.

Dino who?

Dinosaurs roar but unicorns don't.

Knock knock,

Who's there?

Hug.

Hug who?

Will you hug me since I can't hug you?

Knock knock,

Who's there?

Shhhh.

Shhhh who?

Shhhh, it's a magical secret. Only us unicorns can tell you.

Knock knock,

Who's there?

Wish.

Wish who?

Make a special unicorn wish! Maybe it will come true.

Knock knock,

Who's there?

Wish.

Wish who?

I want to wish you a Merry Christmas and a magically unicorn one too!

Knock knock,

Who's there?

I say.

I say who?

Unicorn says, so that's who.

Knock knock,

Who's there?

Salt.

Salt who?

Oh you'll have to add it for me. I don't have fingers.

Knock knock,

Who's there?

How.

How who?

I am great today, how are you?

Knock knock,

Who's there?

Good.

Good who?

We're having a magical day in the clouds, how about you?

Knock knock,

Who's there?

Any.

Any who?

Is anyone home today? No one has let me in, and I am too big to fit.

Knock knock,

Who's there?

Tell.

Tell who?

You'll have to tell them to let us unicorns in.

Knock knock,

Who's there?

Another.

Another who?

Here comes another unicorn knock knock joke just for you.

Knock knock,

Who's there?

Bath.

Bath who?

Do you have any idea how hard it is to give a unicorn a bath?

Knock knock,

Who's there?

Glittery.

Glittery who?

You don't remember me? I'm a glittery unicorn. I live across the street.

Knock knock,

Who's there?

See.

See who?

Can't you see all the unicorns love to play with you?

Knock knock,

Who's there?

Sugar.

Sugar who?

Unicorns love sugar, but we have to remember to eat good things too.

Knock knock,

Who's there?

Remember.

Remember who?

Remember us unicorns always lock our doors.

Knock knock,

Who's there?

Car.

Car who?

A unicorn doesn't need a car. We fly in the sky or run as fast as we can.

Knock knock,

Who's there?

Sugar.

Sugar who?

I came to borrow some sugar.

Knock knock,

Who's there?

Does.

Does who?

So, does this door open or what?

Knock knock,

Who's there?

Bed.

Bed who?

A mermaid sleeps in a bed just like we do.

Knock knock,

Who's there?

Phone.

Phone who?

A mermaid likes to use a cell phone.

Knock knock,

Who's there?

Pepper.

Pepper who?

The pepper made me sneezy again.

Knock knock,

Who's there?

Drums.

Drums who?

Do you know how hard it is for an elephant to play the drums? We have to use our trunk.

Knock knock,

Who's there?

Expensive.

Expensive who?

A goldfish is an expensive fish.

Knock knock,

Who's there?

Your mother.

Your mother who?

Your mother loves you very much.

Knock knock,

Who's there?

Help me.

Help me who?

Help me please, my foot is stuck.

Knock knock,

Who's there?

Cheese.

Cheese who?

Cheeseburgers are so yummy for me and you.

Knock, knock,

Who's there?

Sea horse.

Seahorse who?

The mermaids love to ride their seahorses in the water.

Knock knock,

Who's there?

Reading.

Reading who?

I love reading. Do you love it too?

Knock knock,

Who's there?

Pass the time.

Pass the time who?

I like to pass the time telling knock knock jokes to you.

\-

Knock knock,

Who's there?

Pardon.

Pardon who?

You'll have to pardon my German. I'm still learning.

\-

Knock, knock,

Who's there?

Go back.

Go back who?

Please don't go back on your promise.

\-

Knock knock,

Who's there?

Home.

Home who?

We say that home is most certainly where the heart is.

\-

Knock knock,

Who's there?

Come see.

Come see who?

You have to come see who's at the door.

Knock knock,

Who's there?

Sing.

Sing who?

I feel sad today. Will you sing me a song to cheer me up?

Knock knock,

Who's there?

Good.

Good who?

If you are good today, we can get ice cream on the way home.

Knock knock,

Who's there?

Nice.

Nice who?

Be sure to play nice with your brothers and sisters.

Knock knock,

Who's there?

Rescue.

Rescue who?

Come on! We have to rescue the princess!

Knock knock,

Who's there?

Crown.

Crown who?

The crown needs to go on the king's head.

Knock knock,

Who's there?

Who we are?

Who we are who?

We are awesome just the way we are!

Knock knock,

Who's there?

Apple.

Apple who?

The crab apples are so cute!

Knock knock,

Who's there?

Pistachios.

Pistachios who?

Do you like pistachios as much as I do?

Knock knock,

Who's there?

Smart worm.

Smart worm who?

Did you know a bookworm is a smart worm?

Knock knock,

Who's there?

Miniature golf.

Miniature golf who?

Miniature golf is the best!

Knock knock,

Who's there?

Grandma.

Grandma who?

Do you know how much grandma loves you forever?

Knock knock,

Who's there?

Four.

Four who?

Four apples and five apples make nine apples.

Knock knock,

Who's there?

Pork.

Pork who?

Would you like some pork chops?

Knock knock,

Who's there?

Easy.

Easy who?

My homework was easy to do today.

Knock knock,

Who's there?

Cake.

Cake who?

What kind of cake did you want at your birthday party?

Knock knock,

Who's there?

Strawberry.

Strawberry who?

We're going to have strawberry shortcake at the castle today.

Knock knock,

Who's there?

Ice cream cake.

Ice cream cake who?

The kitty loved having ice cream cake on her birthday!

Knock knock,

Who's there?

Stuffed.

Stuffed who?

The bears can't finish the pie. They're too stuffed!

Knock knock,

Who's there?

Apple.

Apple who?

The worms keep eating the apples before we can.

Knock knock,

Who's there?

Glasses.

Glasses who?

I think the turtle needs glasses. He's not seeing very well.

Knock knock,

Who's there?

Cheese.

Cheese who?

You're eating all the cheese again. You know you have to share.

Knock knock,

Who's there?

Play.

Play who?

Now I have told you, you can't play outside until you finish your homework from mermaid school.

Knock knock,

Who's there?

March.

March who?

We're pretending to be soldiers today. So, we march, march march!

Knock knock,

Who's there?

Navy.

Navy who?

Did you see all the cool ships that they have in the Navy?

Knock knock,

Who's there?

Accident.

Accident who?

I didn't mean to break the lamp. It was an accident.

Knock knock,

Who's there?

Sweet.

Sweet who?

Your teacher is so sweet to all of you.

Knock knock,

Who's there?

Drive.

Drive who?

We were driving and stopped by to say hello to you.

Knock knock,

Who's there?

Bald.

Bald who?

I used to have so much hair, but now I am bald.

Knock knock,

Who's there,

Add.

Add who?

Can you add up everything so that I can have the total, please?

Knock knock,

Who's there?

Careful.

Careful who?

You need to be more careful when playing with children that are younger than you.

Knock knock,

Who's there?

Pizza.

Pizza who?

You didn't save me any of the pizza, did you?

Knock knock,

Who's there?

Roar!

Roar who?

Roar, roar, roar! We are big dinosaurs today!

Knock knock,

Who's there?

Stomp.

Stomp who?

The giants go stomp, stomp, stomp on the ground!

Knock knock,

Who's there?

Dessert.

Dessert who?

You know the rules. You only get dessert after you finish dinner.

Knock knock,

Who's there?

Ginger.

Ginger who?

Gingerbread cookies are a wonderful treat for Christmas.

Knock knock,

Who's there?

Too many.

Too many who?

I ate too many cookies, and now I don't feel good.

Knock knock,

Who's there?

Mommy.

Mommy who?

Mommy will always be here for you.

Knock knock,

Who's there?

Farmers.

Farmers who?

The farmers work really hard to get your food to you.

Knock knock,

Who's there?

Deer.

Deer who?

If you look closely, you can see a dear!

Knock knock,

Who's there?

Sweets.

Sweets who?

You can't eat all those sweets at once. You'll give yourself a tummy ache.

Knock knock,

Who's there?

Doctor's office.

Doctor's office who?

I have to go to the doctor's office today, but I don't want to.

Knock knock,

Who's there?

Park.

Park who?

Do you want to go to the park with us to play today?

Knock knock,

Who's there?

Tell me.

Tell me who?

Can you tell me the truth, please?

Knock, knock,

Who's there?

Sandwich.

Sandwich who?

Please don't eat my sandwich.

Knock knock,

Who's there?

Best.

Best who?

You are my best friend and I love you.

Knock knock,

Who's there?

Meet.

Meet who?

I am very glad to meet you. I have heard wonderful things about you.

Knock knock,

Who's there?

Grandma.

Grandma who?

Grandma said if were good then we can all go play with you.

Knock, knock,

Who's there?

Once.

Once who?

Once upon a time, I saw you at my door, and I opened it for you.

Knock knock,

Who's there?

Married.

Married who?

I am so glad that I got married to you!

Knock knock,

Who's there?

Time.

Time who?

My watch stopped working, and I don't know the time. Do you?

Knock knock,

Who's there?

Tea.

Tea who?

Oh yes, I would love to have some tea with you.

Knock, knock,

Who's there?

Friends.

Friends who?

All of my friends are coming over to play with me today.

Knock, knock,

Who's there?

Catch.

Catch who?

You won't catch me. I am so much faster than you!

Knock knock,

Who's there?

Catch.

Catch who?

Your gonna have to catch up. I am way ahead of you in this race.

Knock knock,

Who's there?

Fall.

Fall who?

If you fall for me, I will fall for you.

Knock knock,

Who's there?

Dreams.

Dreams who?

I will see you in my dreams, and I hope that you will see me in yours.

Knock knock,

Who's there?

Sew.

Sew who?

Would you like to sew a dress with me?

Knock knock,

Who's there?

Dark.

Dark who?

It's too dark in here for me. We need a nightlight.

Knock knock,

Who's there?

Dance.

Dance who?

Get up and dance! Let's have fun!

Knock knock,

Who's there?

Father.

Father who?

Your father will always be there for you.

Knock knock,

Who's there?

Picnic.

Picnic who?

We packed a picnic so that we could eat in the park today and play after.

Knock knock,

Who's there?

Mermaid.

Mermaid who?

I saw a mermaid when I went swimming today!!

Knock knock,

Who's there?

Later.

Later who?

I will see you later on this afternoon.

Knock knock,

Who's there?

Cupcakes.

Cupcakes who?

We're having a cupcake party today and we're inviting you!

Knock knock,

Who's there?

Be.

Be who?

Be prepared is a good motto for people to listen to.

Knock knock,

Who's there?

Listen.

Listen who?

Listen to your heart when it talks to you.

Knock knock,

Who's there?

Happy.

Happy who?

Happy Hanukah from us to you.

Knock knock,

Who's there?

Need.

Need who?

I need a good cup of tea.

Knock knock,

Who's there?

Walls.

Walls who?

Suzy colored all over the walls.

Knock knock,

Who's there?

How many times.

How many times who?

How many times are we going to have to knock on the door before you let us in?

Knock knock,
Who's there?
Tell me.
Tell me who?
Don't worry I already said I was going to tell you.

Knock knock,
Who's there?
Useful.
Useful who?
It would be very useful if you could open the door for us.

Knock knock,
Who's there?
Anniversary.
Anniversary who?
Happy anniversary to you!

Knock knock,
Who's there?
Behavior.
Behavior who?

You need to be on your best behavior today.

Knock knock,

Who's there?

Milkshake.

Milkshake who?

Mermaids love milkshakes after they swim all day.

Knock knock,

Who's there?

Hatch.

Hatch who?

Look the eggs are hatching, and birds are being born.

Knock knock,

Who's there?

Flowers.

Flowers who?

Thank you for the lovely flowers.

Knock knock,

Who's there?

Pineapple.

Pineapple who?

I love pineapples. Do you enjoy them too?

Knock knock,

Who's there?

Shops.

Shops who?

Let's go down to the shops today.

Knock knock,

Who's there?

Finish.

Finish who?

Finish your food then you may be excused.

Knock knock,

Who's there?

School.

School who?

You can't be late to school. You need to finish getting ready.

Knock knock,

Who's there?

Freeze.

Freeze who?

We're going to freeze if you don't let us inside. Will you please open the door?

Knock knock,

Who's there?

Huddle.

Huddle who?

In football, you have to have a huddle.

Knock knock,

Who's there?

Back.

Back who?

I have to go back to work, Be sure that your behaving.

Knock knock,

Who's there?

Cake.

Cake who?

We are baking a chocolate chip cookie cake for your birthday.

Knock knock,

Who's there?

Balance.

Balance who?

My mom does a balancing act with the circus!

Knock knock,

Who's there?

Banana.

Banana who?

Let's all share a banana split!

Knock knock,

Who's there?

Pizza.

Pizza who?

Knock knock,

Who's there?

Pizza.

Pizza who?

Knock knock,

Who's there?

Pizza.

Pizza who?

Knock knock,

Burger.

Burger who?

Well, you didn't want pizza, so I decided to make burgers instead.

Knock knock,

Who's there?

Wool.

Wool who?

I need more wool if you want me to make you that sweater.

Knock knock,

Who's there?

Hero.

Hero who?

Which superhero is your favorite?

Knock knock,

Who's there?

Swimming.

Swimming who?

We're going swimming at the beach today!

Knock knock.

Who's there?

Treehouse.

Treehouse who?

Do you want to build a tree house?

Knock knock,

Who's there?

Pirates.

Pirates who?

The pirates buried the treasure, and now we can't find it.

Knock knock,

Who's there?

Bashful.

Bashful who?

I'm so bashful I can't tell you what I wanted to.

Knock knock,

Who's there?

Home.

Home who?

We better head home it's getting dark.

Knock knock,

Who's there?

Please.

Please who?

Can you please pass me my drink?

Knock knock,

Who's there?

Soon.

Soon who?

Soon things will get better. You will see.

Knock knock,

Who's there?

Balloons.

Balloons who?

I'm blowing up balloons for your birthday party.

Knock knock,

Who's there?

Been.

Been who?

You've been working so hard today.

Knock knock,

Who's there?

Movies.

Movies who?

We haven't been to the movies in a long time. Do you want to go watch one with me?

Knock knock,

Who's there?

Quiet.

Quiet who?

We have to be quiet because we're playing hide and seek. If you're not quiet, they will find our hiding spot.

Knock knock,

Who's there?

Reading.

Reading who?

We are doing reading challenges and they are so much fun!

Knock knock,

Who's there?

Breakfast.

Breakfast who?

Let's have a nice healthy breakfast today.

Knock knock,

Who's there?

Guess.

Guess who?

Guess who I am at your door trying to see and play with you?

Knock knock,

Who's there?

I can't.

I can't who?

I can't play today. I have the flu.

Knock knock,

Who's there?

Forgotten.

Forgotten who?

I think I have forgotten how this joke was supposed to go.

Knock knock,

Who's there?

Baby chickens.

Baby chickens who?

The baby chickens want to come play games with you.

Knock knock,

Who's there?

Bees.

Bees who?

Bees make honey that is sweet to eat.

Knock knock,

Who's there?

Believe.

Believe who?

Believe you! Believe in yourself.

Knock knock,

Who's there?

Been.

Been who?

I've been knocking on your door all morning. Do you not want to see me?

Knock knock,

Who's there?

Monkey.

Monkey who?

Monkeys are sweet and cute just like you!

Knock knock,

Who's there?

Wash.

Wash who?

Before you come to eat wash your hands in the bathroom.

Knock knock,

Who's there?

Dollar.

Dollar who?

I have a dollar that I want to give to you.

Knock knock,

Who's there?

Looks like.

Looks like who?

Looks like I need to go on a diet.

Knock knock,

Who's there?

Christmas.

Christmas who?

I have so many Christmas presents for you!

Knock knock,

Who's there?

I bet.

I bet who?

I bet you don't know who this is knocking on your door.

Knock knock,

Who's there?

Do you know.

Do you know who?

Do you know who I am now?

Knock knock,

Who's there?

Geology.

Geology who?

Geology is so much fun to learn!

Knock knock,

Who's there?

Better.

Better who?

We'd better go grocery shopping.

Knock knock,

Who's there?

Writing.

Writing who?

Writing these knock knock jokes sure is fun!

Knock knock,

Who's there?

Bubblegum.

Bubblegum who?

I sure love bubblegum!

Knock knock,

Who's there?

Shoe.

Shoe who?

Your shoe is on the wrong foot.

Knock knock,

Who's there?

Beautiful.

Beautiful who?

Look at how beautiful the sky looks today.

Knock knock,

Who's there?

Uncle.

Uncle who?

Your aunt and uncle unicorn came this way to see you.

Knock knock,

Who's there?

Santa.

Santa who?

The unicorns found Santa, and he has presents for you.

Knock knock,

Who's there?

Coal.

Coal who?

No one gives coals to the unicorns on Christmas.

Knock knock,

Who's there?

Nickle.

Nickle who?

Grandpa unicorn says nickels used to be worth so much more.

Knock knock,

Who's there?

Blood,

Blood who?

The unicorn vampires want to suck your blood!

Knock knock,

Who's there?

Monster.

Monster who?

Oh that's not a monster. That's a unicorn dressed in costume.

Knock knock,

Who's there

Tie.

Tie who?

The unicorns tied for the race.

Knock knock,

Who's there?

Forgot.

Forgot who?

I forgot which unicorn were supposed to be looking for.

Knock knock,

Who's there?

Can't.

Can't what?

You can't ask me, it's a unicorn secret, and I'm not supposed to tell.

Knock knock,

Who's there?

Stranger.

Stranger who?

Unicorns say never talk to strangers.

Knock knock,

Who's there?

Remember.

Remember who?

You were supposed to remember to bring the unicorns to the game.

Knock knock,

Who's there?

Sick.

Sick who?

Sparkly unicorn had to miss school because she was so sick.

Knock knock,

Who's there?

Birthday.

Birthday who?

The unicorns wish you a happy birthday!

Knock knock,

Who's there?

Walk.

Walk who?

This unicorn would walk a hundred miles to play games with you.

Knock, knock,

Who's there?

Al.

Al who?

Don't worry the unicorns and alligators get along too.

Knock knock,

Who's there?

Starving.

Starving who?

Do you have anything to eat? Unicorns need a lot of food and they're starving again.

Knock knock,

Who's there?

Go.

Go who?

If you go to the door, you'll see seven unicorns here to visit you.

Knock knock,

Who's there?

Bugging.

Bugging who?

Are these unicorn knock knock jokes bothering you?

Knock knock,

Who's there?

Thump, thump.

Thump, thump who?

Thump, thump, thump, the bunny rabbits came to see the unicorns.

Knock knock,

Who's there?

Bee.

Bee who?

Watch out glittery unicorn there is a bee on you.

Knock knock,

Who's there?

Hug.

Hug who?

Funny you should ask. Have you hugged a unicorn yet?

Knock knock,

Who's there?

Letter.

Letter who?

I sent a magical letter to you. Did you receive it yet?

Knock knock,

Who's there?

Tail.

Tail who?

Why do you keep tugging on the poor unicorn's tail?

Knock knock,

Who's there?

Stamp.

Stamp who?

The little unicorns are stamping because they're excited to see you.

Knock knock,

Who's there?

Hide.

Hide who?

You have to find the littlest unicorn. She's hiding from you.

Knock knock,

Who's there?

Two.

Two who?

Two unicorns can play at that game.

Knock knock,

Who's there?

Catch.

Catch who?

You'll have to catch up. The green unicorn is pretty far ahead of you.

Knock knock,

Who's there?

Race.

Race who?

If you race the unicorns, do you think you can win?

Knock knock,

Who's there?

Lying.

Lying who?

Are you lying to Sparkly unicorn? You need to tell the truth.

Knock knock,

Who's there?

Stuffed animals.

Stuffed animals who?

I brought my stuffed animals with me so that we could have a tea party.

Knock knock,

Who's there?

Answer.

Answer who?

Your telephone is ringing so you should answer it. We can hear it outside the door.

Knock knock,

Who's there?

Entire.

Entire who?

Julian ate the entire cake today.

Knock knock,

Who's there?

Chess.

Chess who?

Would you like to play chess with me?

Knock knock,

Who's there?

Kisses.

Kisses who?

Unicorn kisses for you!

Knock knock,

Who's there?

Rain.

Rain who?

Raindrops are falling on my mane and getting it wet.

Knock knock,

Who's there?

Miss.

Miss who?

Do you miss your unicorn because she misses you?

Knock knock,

Who's there?

Sparkles.

Sparkles who?

Sparks the unicorn is sparkling for you.

Knock knock,

Who's there?

Boo.

Boo who?

Oh, sweetheart unicorns aren't scary. Don't be frightened.

Knock knock,

Who's there?

Karate.

Karate who?

Unicorn karate chop!

Knock knock,

Who's there?

Wanna.

Wanna who?

Wanna play hide and seek? My sparkly horn makes me easy to find.

Knock knock,

Who's there?

Rainbow.

Rainbow horn of the unicorn!

Knock knock,

Who's there?

Untied.

Untied who?

Your shoelaces are untied.

Knock knock,

Who's there?

First.

First who?

Today is the first day of flying season for unicorns.

Knock knock,

Who's there?

Play.

Play who?

Would you like to play with us unicorns today?

Knock knock,

Who's there?

Checkers.

Checkers who?

If chess isn't your game, would you like to play checkers?

Knock knock,

Who's there?

Trumpet.

Trumpet who?

I can't play the trumpet; I'm a goose.

Knock knock,

Who's there?

Food.

Food who?

Be careful not to touch the food. It's still too hot to touch just now.

Knock knock,

Who's there?

Sushi.

Sushi who?

Do you want to get some sushi? Its super yummy for your tummy.

Knock knock,

Who's there?

Help.

Help who?

I think you need help opening the door because its stuck on my foot.

Knock knock,

Who's there?

Old.

Old who?

It's your old friend Joseph at the door. You remember me, don't you?

Knock knock,

Who's there?

Voice.

Voice who?

You can't recognize the sound of my voice?

Knock knock,

Who's there?

Remember.

Remember who?

You will remember me when you see my face.

Knock knock,

Who's there?

Santa.

Santa who?

Santa came and brought presents for all of us today.

Knock knock,

Who's there?

Just a second.

Just a second who?

Just a second, I am finishing my homework.

Knock knock,

Who's there?

Lovely.

Lovely who?

It's a lovely day, and we would like to share it with you.

Knock knock,

Who's there?

Beautiful.

Beautiful who?

You look so beautiful today!

Knock knock,

Who's there?

Handsome.

Handsome who?

You look so handsome today!

Knock knock,

Who's there?

Questions.

Questions who?

You ask a lot of questions, don't you?

Knock knock,

Who's there?

Good.

Good who?

So far everything is going well!

Knock knock,

Who's there?

The same.

The same who?

It's the same person who's been knocking on the door all day silly.

Knock knock,

Who's there?

Someday.

Someday who?

I bet you someday when I come to your door, you'll recognize me and I won't have to knock.

Knock knock,

Who's there?

Email.

Email who?

Santa sent you an email, but you never wrote back to him.

Knock knock,

Who's there?

Navy.

Navy who?

The Navy has entire fleets of submarines.

Knock knock,

Who's there?

Three.

Three who?

Three little unicorns playing in your kitchen.

Knock knock,

Who's there?

Glad.

Glad who?

Aren't you glad the weekend is here? Now you and the unicorns can play all day.

Knock knock,

Who's there?

Great.

Great day.

The unicorns had a great day playing magical games with you.

Knock knock,

Who's there?

Wonderful.

Wonderful who?

Our friend Pinky the unicorn had a great time with you.

Knock knock,

Who's there?

Hippo.

Hippo who?

Hippopotamus's love hanging out with unicorns.

Knock knock,
Who's there?
Why.
Why who?
Why is it always me that's having to try and knock on the door? I'm a unicorn. I don't even have fingers.

Knock knock,
Who's there?
Run.
Run who?
If you run with us, our magic will lift you higher!

Knock knock,
Who's there?
Sore.
Sore who?
My snout is sore from trying to knock so much.

Knock knock,
Who's there?
Bell.
Bell who?

Is your bell working? Two unicorns tried to ring it, and you can't hear it at all?

Knock knock,

Who's there?

How many.

How many who?

How many unicorns does it take to screw in a lightbulb?

None silly. Unicorns don't have fingers.

Knock knock,

Who's there?

Cry.

Cry who?

The unicorns are crying because you won't let them in to play with you.

Knock knock,

Who's there?

Dinner.

Dinner who?

It's time for dinner, and the unicorns will get their cupcakes.

Knock knock,

Who's there?

Excuse me.

Excuse me who?

Excuse me, would you mind scooting over your sitting on my tail.

Knock knock,

Who's there?

Kangaroo.

Kangaroo who?

The kangaroos are coming to join the unicorns on their picnic today.

Knock knock,

Who's there?

Surprise.

Surprise who?

Glittery unicorn, pink, and blue all came to see you.

Knock knock,

Who's there?

Party.

Party who?

The unicorns are having a tea and cake party. Would you like to come too?

Knock knock,

Who's there?

Puppets.

Puppets who?

I brought all my puppets to have a party with you.

Knock knock,

Who's there?

Sing.

Sing who?

I am going to sing my favorite songs to you.

Knock knock,

Who's there?

Flute.

Flute who?

Ducks can't play the flute. Their bills are too big.

Knock knock,

Who's there?

Friends.

Friends who?

Your friends came by to see you, but you were asleep.

Knock knock,

Who's there?

Nap time.

Nap time who?

You need to take a nap before you go play with your friends today.

Who's there?

Knock knock,

Who's there?

Mommy.

Mommy who?

My mommy braided my hair so it wouldn't get in my face while I played.

Knock knock,

Who's there?

Doctor.

Doctor who?

We need a doctor. Can we count on you?

Knock knock,

Who's there?

Snacks.

Snacks who?

We have snacks and cookies for you today.

Knock knock,

Who's there?

Music.

Music who?

I love listening to music when I am hanging out with my friends.

Knock knock,

Who's there?

Sandwiches.

Sandwiches who?

We're eating healthy sandwiches while we're having lunch today.

Knock knock,

Who's there?

Unicorn school.

Unicorn school who?

Don't you remember, we have unicorn school today?

Knock knock,

Who's there?

Halloween candy.

Halloween candy who?

I think us unicorns ate all the Halloween candy without you.

Knock knock,

Who's there?

Treat.

Treat who?

I get unicorn treats this Halloween!

Knock knock,

Who's there?

Wrong.

Wrong who?

I think this unicorn has the wrong door.

Knock knock,

Who's there?

Presents.

Presents who?

Open up. Us unicorns have magical presents for you today!

Knock knock,

Who's there?

See.

See who?

Can't you see all the unicorns love to play with you?

Knock knock,

Who's there?

Sugar.

Sugar who?

Unicorns love sugar, but we have to remember to eat good things too.

Knock knock,

Who's there?

Remember.

Remember who?

Remember us unicorns always lock our doors.

Knock knock,

Who's there?

Car.

Car who?

A unicorn doesn't need a car. We fly in the sky or run as fast as we can.

Knock knock,

Who's there?

Someday.

Someday who?

Someday our magical friends will come.

Knock knock,

Who's there?

Feed.

Feed who?

We have to remember to feed all of us unicorns before bedtime.

Knock knock,

Who's there?

Storytime.

Storytime who?

Gather around so that we can read stories. It's story time!

Knock knock,

Who's there?

Hippos.

Hippos who?

Hippos love to play in the water!

Knock knock,

Who's there?

Hippos.

Hippos who?

Hippity hoppity hippos!!

Knock knock,

Who's there?

Friendship.

Friendship who?

Our friendship is so important to me.

Knock knock,

Who's there?

Mice.

Mice who?

Mice love cheese!

Knock knock,

Who's there?

Movies.

Movies who?

We had popcorn and candy when we went to the movies today.

Knock knock,

Who's there?

Necklace.

Necklace who?

I bought you a necklace for your birthday today.

Knock knock,

Who's there?

Bounce.

Bounce who?

I love to bounce the ball. Bounce, bounce, bounce!!

Knock knock,

Who's there?

Clowns.

Clowns who?

I love how clowns are so funny and colorful!

Knock knock,

Who's there?

Cold.

Cold who?

It's cold enough for snow now.

Knock knock,

Who's there?

Kitty.

Kitty who?

My kitty cat is really happy to see you!

Knock knock,

Who's there?

Yarn.

Yarn who?

I need more yarn if I am going to be finishing these socks for you.

Knock knock,

Who's there?

Dog.

Dog who?

My dog can jump as high as you!

Knock knock,

Who's there?

Bundle.

Bundle who?

Be sure to bundle up.

It's cold today.

Knock knock,

Who's there?

Snowman.

Snowman who?

My snowman is going to be a magic part of Christmas.

Knock knock,

Who's there?

Coconut.

Coconut who?

We're not coconuts.

Knock knock,

Who's there?

I wanna see.

I wanna see who?

I wanna see my family, friends, and you.

Knock knock,

Who's there?

Package.

Package who?

There's a package outside the door for you.

Knock knock,

Who's there?

Love.

Love who?

We all love you so much.

Knock knock,

Who's there?

You know.

You know who?

You know who you are.

Knock knock,

Who's there?

Mermaid fins.

Mermaid fins who?

Did you know a mermaid's fins are bigger than you?

\-

Knock knock,

Who's there?

Coffee.

Coffee who?

We brought coffee and doughnuts for you.

\-

Knock knock,

Who's there?

Blue.

Blue who?

Don't be blue. We've got presents for you!

\-

Knock knock,

Who's there?

Mermaid speed.

Mermaid speed who?

Mermaid speed in the water is faster than we can see!

\-

Knock knock,

Who's there?

Crown.

Crown who?

You have to give the crown back to the Queen.

Knock knock,

Who's there?

Last.

Last who?

This is the last of the knock knock jokes.

Knock knock,

Who's there?

One more.

One more who?

Just kidding! There's one more knock knock joke.

Conclusion

Thanks for making it through to the end of *Karen's Knock Knock Jokes for Kids - The Unbreakable Door That No One Ever Got Past*. Let's hope it was entertaining and provided you with a few hours of excitement as you worked through the jokes.

Remember to claim your free book (Link at the front of the book) and also check out our other books that can be found on our Facebook page www.facebook.com/bluesourceandfriends.

Finally, if you found this book useful in any way, a review on Amazon is always appreciated!

Karen J. Bun

Karen's Unicorn Knock Knock Jokes

The Magical Door That Spurts Rainbow Endlessly

Karen J. Bun

Contents

Introduction 399

Bluesource And Friends 406

Unicorn Knock Knock Jokes! 407

Conclusion 526

© Copyright 2019 by Bluesource And Friends - All rights reserved.

The following eBook is reproduced below with the goal of providing information that is as accurate and reliable as possible. Regardless, purchasing this eBook can be seen as consent to the fact that both the publisher and the author of this book are in no way experts on the topics discussed within and that any recommendations or suggestions that are made herein are for entertainment purposes only. Professionals should be consulted as needed prior to undertaking any of the action endorsed herein.

This declaration is deemed fair and valid by both the American Bar Association and the Committee of Publishers Association and is legally binding throughout the United States.

Furthermore, the transmission, duplication, or reproduction of any of the following work including specific information will be considered an illegal act irrespective of if it is done electronically or in print. This extends to creating a secondary or tertiary copy of the work or a recorded copy and is only allowed with the express written consent from the Publisher. All additional right reserved.

The information in the following pages is broadly considered a truthful and accurate account of facts and as such, any inattention, use, or misuse of the information in question by the reader will render any resulting actions solely under their purview. There are no scenarios in which the publisher or the original author of this work can be in any fashion deemed liable for any hardship or damages that may befall them after undertaking information described herein.

Additionally, the information in the following pages is intended only for informational purposes and should thus be thought of as universal. As befitting its nature, it is presented without assurance regarding its prolonged validity or interim quality. Trademarks that are mentioned are done without written consent and can in no way be considered an endorsement from the trademark holder.

Introduction

Unicorns have long since been the favorite of little girls and teenagers everywhere, and a lot of people have fallen in love with the magical realms of wonder unicorns represent. They represent the worlds that our imaginations can lead us to and endless possibilities of the magical and wondrous things that we can see and learn about. Unicorns are such beautiful and wondrous creatures, and every girl wants to have one as a pet or collect as many items with the unicorn on them as possible. Unicorns are beautiful mythical animals that have a horse-like body, though they're not considered actual horses because of the horn they have on their forehead. This horn has had many legends told about it almost rivaling the stories and legends told about the unicorn itself.

The horn has been said to heal the sick and have other healing properties as well. This is the main story about the horn, though there have been many other stories about the horn. It has kept people fascinated with unicorns, and the stories and legends behind them have been around for years.

They are legendary creatures that are known for their strength and loyalty. They are said to be very strong, and that is why some cultures love them so much. They view them as an untouchable creature and a source of pure strength, which, in turn, inspired cultures to be immovably strong as well. Some cultures love unicorns so much that there are actually days dedicated to them, including whole days of unicorn celebration and fun with unicorn-themed events. They also had coins with unicorns on them as well in other cultures.

There have also been some really popular films for children and adults featuring unicorns. These films have made unicorns even more popular than they were before. Another neat thing is that the pop culture phenomenon that stemmed from the love of unicorns has actually given birth to memes and gifs. Living in a digital age, as we do, social media can't be avoided, so the love for unicorns exploded further once the internet took hold of the unicorn craze as well.

There have even been bands named after the mythical creature. It was very disappointing to their fans that they didn't last very long. They were around for only about four years in total and only produced one album. However, at least, their following got to hear them play for a little while before they disbanded, and they even had a cult following.

Thanks to this popular creation, they have also had a massive school supply following as well. Everything from notebooks, stickers, memo pads, you name it, you can find a unicorn on it. They've also expanded into makeup tutorials and hair tutorials, even delving into cosplay. Many kids and families all over the world have at least one or more objects in their house that depict unicorns and will admit that it brightens up their home while making the inhabitants happy.

Most unicorns have been said to either have purple eyes or a sky blue pair of eyes. Their bodies can be of any color, and they have different names for these unicorns as well. But, one thing that most agree on is that its eyes are one of those two colors. One of the cutest facts about unicorns is that they call the baby unicorns a sparkle. As children love sparkles and glitter and everything in between, this is one of the reasons that children love little unicorns. They are known for being cute and adorable, which, of course, children love because they are drawn to all things cute and adorable.

They are nearly impossible to catch, and that's why most people don't see very many of them and that you won't be able to find them in most places. They are not only impossible to catch, but also, they are incredibly rare. People have said that they have seen them in real life or at least thought that they have with confirmed sightings. Some of these people include famous politicians or dictators.

The rarity and purity of these creatures have been shown in many popular movies as of late. These movies show that the creatures are pure and innocent and that these amazing creatures should be treated with respect and have to be viewed as amazingly unique, specifically ones with magical places and students. Because these movies were so popular, millions of people who saw these movies began to see unicorns in a new light once again. This gave a massive boost to the unicorn popularity, and people began wanting as many unicorn objects they could get their hands on.

Sales of unicorn memorabilia once again spiked as people fell in love with unicorns again, and now, it's evolved into a phenomenon. While in the movies they are usually depicted as pearly white, studies show that they can be any color.

As unicorns are amazingly popular and awesome creatures, children love seeing the wonderful animal on television and getting to experience magic. These jokes are all about these magical creatures, so we can have a good laugh while learning about them. This book will be full of knock-knock jokes designed to make you laugh and have fun reading a great book.

Knock-knock jokes have been around for ages, bringing delight and joy to those who hear them every day. Children giggle and have fun and feel closer or connected to the person telling the joke and often repeat it for all their friends to hear because they believe that it is so funny. They can make people laugh after a hard day or cheer someone up when they are sick or feeling down. They have been around since about the early twentieth century, and they are a staple of American humor.

The great thing about these jokes is that they can be understood by kids and adults alike. No matter what your age is, there is a knock-knock joke out there for you, and even if you can't find one, you'll still be able to grasp the concept of each one. This makes it great for people of all ages to feel closer to each other and laugh together. However, because everyone has a different view on things, not all people could possibly enjoy a single joke together, it's still something that you can share with others and enjoy as well.

As they began to gain popularity, they could be heard just about everywhere with people making up new jokes every day. Businesses even held knock-knock joke contests because they became so popular and had people flocking to them because they enjoyed them so much. Some orchestras even added knock-knock jokes into their musical set because they thought that it would add something to the performance that they were giving. Radio stations would also play jokes on air. There were some that, during political campaigning times, would play all day.

It was everywhere you turned around. Grocery stores even printed them in their ads to drum up business in their stores because the jokes were gaining so much attention with the masses and they wanted more people to come to them. Soon after the craze started, knock-knock clubs arose, and soon after, people began singing songs about knock-knock jokes as well. It's even been guessed that Shakespeare wrote a few knock-knock jokes in his plays. Some of them appeared in his most famous plays, which were read by the masses every day in some cases.

They did lose traction for a little while during certain political campaigns, and it looked like they might be phased out as a negative stigma arrived from knock-knock jokes. Fortunately, they weren't, and the jokes lived another day with books beginning to fly off the shelves again at bookstores or library shelves as people started to read and discover them again. Once this happened, people realized that, while they were famous, it was still hit or miss. This makes sense because everyone is different and has their own sense of humor. So, there are some that like them and some that are still skeptical about the scale of their funniest jokes, but most people can agree that they think knock-knock jokes are funny and a great way to spend time laughing and enjoying the company of others who like them as well. A knock-knock joke, for those who don't know, is a question and answer joke. Mostly, for kids these days, there are a few exceptions. Basically, what happens is that you ask a question, and then, the other person answers. You add your answer and then finish the joke. Versatile as they are funny, knock-knock jokes can be told at any occasion because there are jokes for every holiday, from Christmas to Halloween or Thanksgiving, and there are jokes for just about anything. You can make knock-knock jokes about animals, or food, life, jobs, or teachers. You can make up knock-knock jokes on literally any subject, but the fun part is seeing just how many subjects you can actually find jokes on.

They've been put in everything from books to movies, and whether you're a fan of knock-knock jokes or not, they're here to stay. Authors have sold millions of books on knock-knock jokes because children love them so much and most people are fond of them and think they're absolutely delightful and funny.

This book covers a variety of topics with our unicorn jokes to make you laugh out loud and have fun while reading, which is a win-win situation on both accounts. This also helps children who don't necessarily like reading. Most children like to read things that make them laugh and get them interested, which is why we have funny unicorn jokes in this book.

Bluesource And Friends

This book is brought to you by Bluesource And Friends, a happy book publishing company.

Our motto is **"Happiness Within Pages"**

We promise to deliver amazing value to readers with our books.

We also appreciate honest book reviews from our readers.

Connect with us on our Facebook page

www.facebook.com/bluesourceandfriends and stay tuned to our latest book promotions and free giveaways.

Don't forget to claim your FREE book

https://tinyurl.com/karenbrainteasers

Also check out our bestseller book

https://tinyurl.com/lateralthinkingpuzzles

Unicorn Knock Knock Jokes!

Knock, knock!

Who's there?

Corn.

Corn who?

UNICORN!!!

Knock, knock!

Who's there?

Unique.

Unique who?

UNIQUE UNICORN!!

Knock, knock!

Who's there?

Rainbow.

Rainbow who?

The rainbow unicorn!

Knock, knock!

Who's there?

Corn.

Corn who?

Unicorn jokes are pretty corny, huh?

Knock, knock!
Who's there?
Flying.
Flying who?
Flying unicorn right above you!

Knock, knock!
Who's there?
Rainbow.
Rainbow who?
Rainbow unicorns are the best!

Knock, knock!
Who's there?
Candy.
Candy who?
Did you let the unicorn eat all my candy again?

Knock, knock!
Who's there?
Happy.
Happy who?
The unicorn's say happy birthday to you!

Knock, knock!

Who's there?

Lion.

Lion who?

You're not trying to lie to a unicorn, are you?

Knock, knock!

Who's there?

Thank you.

Thank you who?

Thank you for being the unicorn's best friend.

Knock, knock!

Who's there?

Hooves.

Hooves who?

Unicorns have strong hooves for racing.

Knock, knock!

Who's there?

Ready.

Ready who?

Ready set go! Unicorn race!!

Knock, knock!
Who's there?
Kisses.
Kisses who?
Unicorn kisses for you!

Knock, knock!
Who's there?
Rain.
Rain who?
Raindrops are falling on my mane and getting it wet.

Knock, knock!
Who's there?
Miss.
Miss who?
Do you miss your unicorn because she misses you?

Knock, knock!
Who's there?
Sparkles.
Sparkles who?
Sparkles, the unicorn, is sparkling for you.

Knock, knock!

Who's there?

Boo.

Boo who?

Oh, sweetheart unicorns aren't scary. Don't be frightened.

Knock, knock!

Who's there?

Karate.

Karate who?

Unicorn karate chop!

Knock, knock!

Who's there?

Wanna.

Wanna who?

Wanna play hide and seek? My sparkly horn makes me easy to find.

Knock, knock!

Who's there?

Rainbow.

Rainbow who?

Rainbow horn of the unicorn!

Knock, knock!

Who's there?

Ho, ho.

Ho, ho who?

Ho, ho, ho is Santa. He and I are best friends.

Knock, knock!

Who's there?

Door.

Door who?

The door's too small for a unicorn to fit through.

Knock, knock!

Who's there?

Chocolate.

Chocolate who?

Of course, unicorns love chocolate!

Knock, knock!

Who's there?

Untied.

Untied who?

Your shoelaces are untied.

No, unicorns don't have shoes!

Knock, knock!

Who's there?

First.

First who?

Today is the first day of flying season for unicorns.

Knock, knock!

Who's there?

Play.

Play who?

Would you like to play with us unicorns today?

Knock, knock!

Who's there?

Unicorn.

Unicorn who?

How many unicorns do you know silly?

Knock, knock!

Who's there?

Remember.

Remember who?

Remember your unicorn friend!

Knock, knock!

Who's there?

Crown.

Crown who?

My mane makes a rainbow crown around my head.

Knock, knock!

Who's there?

Unicorn.

Unicorn who?

Unicorns sparkle like pretty diamonds.

Knock, knock!

Who's there?

Bite.

Bite who?

Don't worry, I won't bite you. You're not what unicorns eat.

Knock, knock!

Who's there?

Favorite.

Favorite who?

A unicorn's favorite food is rainbow nuggets!

Knock, knock!

Who's there?

Favorite too.

Favorite too who?

A unicorn's other favorite food is unicorn bites.

Knock, knock!

Who's there?

Outside.

Outside who?

We were all outside looking for you.

Knock, knock!

Who's there?

Heard.

Heard who?

The unicorns heard you were home and came to visit you!

Knock, knock!

Who's there?

I can.

I can who?

I bet I can tell more unicorn knock-knock jokes than you.

Knock, knock!

Who's there?

Please.

Please who?

Will you come and play with me and my unicorn friends please?

Knock, knock!

Who's there?

Merry.

Merry who?

Merry Christmas from all of us unicorns to you!

Knock, knock!

Who's there?

Holly.

Holly who?

Holly jolly holidays from our unicorns to you.

Knock, knock!

Who's there?

How.

How who?

You must know. It's your special rainbow friend knocking.

Knock, knock!

Who's there?

I.

I who?

Your unicorn friend is here.

Knock, knock!

Who's there?

You.

You who?

You are here to play with us unicorns in the clouds.

Knock, knock!

Who's there?

Be.

Be who?

Be your amazing unicorn sparkly self.

Knock, knock!

Who's there?

You.

You who?

My special unicorn eyes see you!

Knock, knock!

Who's there?

Me.

Me who?

You see me with your extra special eyes!

Knock, knock!

Who's there?

Owl.

Owl who?

Did you know the owls fly alongside the unicorns too?

Knock, knock!

Who's there?

I.

I who?

I love you, my special unicorn.

Knock, knock!

Who's there?

Moo.

Moo who?

Unicorns don't say moo.

Knock, knock!

Who's there?

Atch.

Atch who?

Ugh oh, when a unicorn sneezes, glitter sprays everywhere. I'll need a big tissue!

Knock, knock!

Who's there?

Pee.

Pee who?

Peekaboo! My special eyes have landed on you!

Knock, knock!

Who's there?

Beat.

Beat who?

Let's listen to a great beat as we fly high in the sky.

Knock, knock!

Who's there?

Adore.

Adore who?

Unicorns all adore you!

Knock, knock!

Who's there?

Bee.

Bee who?

The honeybees can fly with us too.

Knock, knock!

Who's there?

Business.

Business who?

Unicorn official business.

Knock, knock!

Who's there?

Remember.

Remember who?

Remember all the unicorns are unique, just like you.

Knock, knock!

Who's there?

Thank you.

Thank you who?

Thank you for letting us make magical memories with you.

Knock, knock!

Who's there?

Ready.

Ready who?

Ready set run!!

Knock, knock!

Who's there?

Better.

Better who?

I hope the purple unicorn feels better soon.

Knock, knock!

Who's there?

Alphabet.

Alphabet who?

Alphabet soup. We, unicorns, are great spellers.

Knock, knock!

Who's there?

How.

How who?

How are you I heard one of the unicorns is blue?

Knock, knock!

Who's there?

Glitter.

Glitter who?

Unicorns are famous for being glittery too!

Knock, knock!

Who's there?

Me.

Me who?

I'm standing right in front of you with a rainbow tail. Surely you can't miss me, right?

Knock, knock!

Who's there?

Alias.

Alias who?

I am sorry, I don't think that the unicorns know you.

Knock, knock!

Who's there?

Boo.

Boo who?

Oh sweetheart, don't be scared. Unicorns are super friendly.

Knock, knock!

Who's there?

Stuck.

Stuck who?

Your door is stuck, and I can't fit my hooves inside.

Knock, knock!

Who's there?

Love.

Love who?

Do you love your rainbow friend? We all love you.

Knock, knock!

Who's there?

Cashew.

Cashew who?

Do you like cashews? This unicorn likes peanuts.

Knock, knock!

Who's there?

Pen.

Pen who?

I don't need a pen. Unicorns can't write.

Knock, knock!

Who's there?

Come on.

Come on who?

Come on and play with us. We're playing rainbow speed races!

Knock, knock!

Who's there?

Who.

Who who?

I'm sorry unicorns can't speak owl.

Knock, knock!

Forget.

Forget who?

Forget no one. Remember all of the unicorn friends of yours.

Knock, knock!

Who's there?

Remember.

Remember who?

Do you remember playing unicorn games with me?

Knock, knock!

Who's there?

Sure.

Sure who?

We, magical beings, sure do love you.

Knock, knock!

Who's there?

Don't.

Don't who?

Don't you want to invite us in? We, unicorns, get cold easily.

Knock, knock!

Who's there?

Where?

Where who?

Where did you go? I've got four unicorns looking for you!

Knock, knock!

Who's there?

Don't.

Don't who?

I don't want to go to unicorn school without you.

Knock, knock!

Who's there?

Please.

Please who?

Please join us for unicorn games. It will be no fun without you.

Knock, knock!

Who's there?

Whatcha?

Whatcha who?

Whatcha doing today? Are you going to come braid unicorn hair?

Knock, knock!

Who's there?

In time.

In time who?

You made it just in time for unicorn cake!

Knock, knock!

Who's there?

How.

How who?

How are you sure it's not another unicorn knocking?

Knock, knock!

Who's there?

Unicorn school.

Unicorn school who?

Don't you remember we have unicorn school today?

Knock, knock!

Who's there?

Halloween candy.

Halloween candy who?

I think us unicorns ate all the Halloween candy without you.

Knock, knock!

Who's there?

Treat.

Treat who?

I get unicorn treats this Halloween!

Knock, knock!

Who's there?

Wrong.

Wrong who?

I think this unicorn has the wrong door.

Knock, knock!

Who's there?

Presents.

Presents who?

Open up. We, unicorns, have magical presents for you today!

Knock, knock!

Who's there?

Crystal unicorn.

Crystal unicorn who?

Did you know my crystal unicorn eyes see you?

Knock, knock!

Who's there?

Let.

Let who?

Let me in so we can play glitter races!

Knock, knock!

Who's there?

I win.

I win who?

I won the glitter races, so unfortunately you lose.

Knock, knock!

Who's there?

Dino.

Dino who?

Dinosaurs roar but unicorns don't.

Knock, knock!

Who's there?

Hug.

Hug who?

Will you hug me since I can't hug you?

Knock, knock!

Who's there?

Shhhh.

Shhhh who?

Shhhh, it's a magical secret. Only we, unicorns, can tell you.

Knock, knock!
Who's there?
Wish.
Wish who?
Make a special unicorn wish! Maybe it will come true.

Knock, knock!
Who's there?
Wish.
Wish who?
I want to wish you a merry Christmas and a magically unicorn one too!

Knock, knock!
Who's there?
I say.
I say who?
Unicorn says so that's who.

Knock, knock!
Who's there?
Salt.
Salt who?
Oh you'll have to add it for me. I don't have fingers.

Knock, knock!

Who's there?

How.

How who?

I am great today, how are you?

Knock, knock!

Who's there?

Good.

Good who?

We're having a magical day in the clouds. How about you?

Knock, knock!

Who's there?

Any.

Any who?

Is anyone home today? No one has let me in and I am too big to fit.

Knock, knock!

Who's there?

Tell.

Tell who?

You'll have to tell them to let us unicorns in.

Knock, knock!

Who's there?

Another.

Another who?

Here comes another unicorn knock-knock joke just for you.

Knock, knock!

Who's there?

Bath.

Bath who?

Do you have any idea how hard it is to give a unicorn a bath?

Knock, knock!

Who's there?

Glittery.

Glittery who?

Don't remember me? I'm Glittery the unicorn. I live across the street.

Knock, knock!

Who's there?

See.

See who?

Can't you see all the unicorns love to play with you?

Knock, knock!

Who's there?

Sugar.

Sugar who?

Unicorns love sugar but we have to remember to eat good things too.

Knock, knock!

Who's there?

Remember.

Remember who?

Remember us unicorns always lock our doors.

Knock, knock!

Who's there?

Car.

Car who?

A unicorn doesn't need a car. We fly in the sky or run as fast as we can.

Knock, knock!

Who's there?

Someday.

Someday who?

Someday our magical friends will come.

Knock, knock!

Who's there?

Feed.

Feed who?

We have to remember to feed all of us unicorns before bedtime.

Knock, knock!

Who's there?

Mountain.

Mountain who?

We're all playing on the mountain today leaving rainbows and sunshine behind.

Knock, knock!

Who's there?

Laughing.

Laughing who?

Are you laughing at these unicorn knock-knock jokes, too?

Knock, knock!

Who's there?

Doctor.

Doctor who?

Oh no, did one of the unicorns need a doctor again?

Knock, knock!

Who's there?

The same.

The same who?

The same unicorn that knocked the last time, can't you recognize me?

Knock, knock!

Who's there?

Roof.

Roof who?

The roof is leaking, we need to fix it. It makes our mane stick to our backs.

Knock, knock!

Who's there?

Read.

Read who?

Of course unicorns can read. It's good for you.

Knock, knock!

Who's there?

Read.

Read who?

You got to keep reading these unicorn jokes.

Knock, knock!

Who's there?

Ring.

Ring who?

A ring around the roses, all the unicorns dancing and prancing around the roses.

Knock, knock!

Who's there?

Run.

Run who?

Let's run another marathon together!

Knock, knock!

Who's there?

Sat.

Sat who?

My friends and I sat on your phone. Sorry you couldn't call the rest of the unicorns.

Knock, knock!

Who's there?

Row.

Row who?

Row, row, row, your boat gently down the… Hey, wait a minute! Unicorns don't fit in boats.

Knock, knock!

Who's there?

Rain.

Rain who?

It's raining unicorns and kittens out here today!

Knock, knock!

Who's there?

Bell.

Bell who?

You couldn't ring the bell, could you? No hands.

Knock, knock!

Who's there?

Prance.

Prance who?

I love to prance and run about with my unicorn friends.

Knock, knock!

Who's there?

Clean.

Clean who?

I just had a bath. My mane and tail are so shiny!

Knock, knock!
Who's there?
Roll with.
Roll with who?
Roll with the punches.
I can't punch remember? I have hooves.

Knock, knock!
Who's there?
Chair.
Chair who?
Would you like to sit down?
Oh, no, thank you, but unicorns prefer to stand.

Knock, knock!
Who's there?
Who.
Who who?
You owls are early, we are not supposed to fly till the suns out.

Knock, knock!
Who's there?
Whinny.
Whinny who?
Just whinny if you understand me.

Knock, knock!
Who's there?
Money.
Money who?
Even unicorn money doesn't grow on trees you know.

Knock, knock!
Who's there?
Mind.
Mind who?
Unicorns are very good at minding their manners.

Knock, knock!
Who's there?
Mind.
Mind who?
You need to make up your mind about which rainbow we are flying to today.

Knock, knock!
Who's there?
Merrily,
Merrily who?

Merrily, merrily, merrily, merrily, for unicorn's life is but a magical dream.

Knock, knock!
Who's there?
Look out.
Look out who?
Look out, because here comes another unicorn knock-knock joke for you to enjoy.

Knock, knock!
Who's there?
Look.
Look who?
Even unicorns look before they leap.

Knock, knock!
Who's there?
Let's go.
Let's go who?
We need to go before we are late. Unicorns like to be on time.

Knock, knock!
Who's there?
Lean.

Lean who?

Lean in and I will tell you a magical secret.

Knock, knock!

Who's there?

Lonely.

Lonely who?

Unicorns get lonely without their friends with them.

Knock, knock!

Who's there?

Coat.

Coat who?

Would you like to hang up your coat?

I can't. It is attached to my body.

Knock, knock!

Who's there?

Cream.

Cream who?

Us unicorns are the cream of the crop, don't you know?

Knock, knock!

Who's there?

Cell.

Cell who?

I know you have hooves, but here's my cell if you need it.

Knock, knock!

Who's there?

Time.

Time who?

It's time for dinner, guys. Hope we have enough room at the table for six unicorns.

Knock, knock!

Who's there?

Open.

Open who?

Your door was open, but I knocked with my snout to be polite.

Knock, knock!

Who's there?

Hip.

Hip who?

My buddies and I are joined at the hip.

Knock, knock!

Who's there?

Where.

Where who?

Where are all of the unicorns playing today?

Knock, knock!

Who's there?

Eggs.

Eggs who?

Do unicorns eat eggs and bacon in the morning?

Knock, knock!

Who's there?

Bike.

Bike who?

Unicorns can't ride bikes. We will fly beside you.

Knock, knock!

Who's there?

I knew.

I knew who?

I knew it was my special friend at the door.

Knock, knock!

Who's there?

Pickle.

Pickle who?

I would like a pickle to share with my blue unicorn.

Knock, knock!

Who's there?

Clue.

Clue who?

I have no clue where the other unicorns went. Do you?

Knock, knock!

Who's there?

Mischievous.

Mischievous who?

Unicorns love to play. They are so mischievous in their ways.

Knock, knock!

Who's there?

Lost.

Lost who?

Make sure the unicorns don't get lost when you play outside today.

Knock, knock!

Who's there?

Cupcakes.

Cupcakes who?

Unicorns love cupcakes with extra sprinkles!

Knock, knock!

Who's there?

This way.

This way who?

The unicorns are hiding. You go this way and I'll go that way, so we can find them.

Knock, knock!

Who's there?

Pink.

Pink who?

I don't think the pink unicorn is here. I will have to visit her later.

Knock, knock!

Who's there?

Driving,

Driving who?

Unicorns don't drive. We will run next to you.

Knock, knock!

Who's there?

All.

All who?

All is not lost. We unicorns still have our friends and family and each other.

Knock, knock!
Who's there?
Together.
Together who?
We, unicorns, are all in this together.

Knock, knock!
Who's there?
Hello.
Hello who?
I'm the rainbow unicorn. My name is not hello.

Knock, knock!
Who's there?
Hot.
Hot who?
We, unicorns, need to cool down. It's too hot for us today.

Knock, knock!
Who's there?
How many.
How many who?

How many times will we, unicorns, need to repeat ourselves to you?

Knock, knock!

Who's there?

When.

When who?

Flying the magical waves of the ocean was fun today. When can we do it again?

Knock, knock!

Who's there?

Generally.

Generally who?

Generally, I do not tell such funny unicorn knock-knock jokes.

Knock, knock!

Who's there?

Afraid.

Afraid who?

Are unicorns afraid of the big bad wolf?

Knock, knock!

Who's there?

Exhausted.

Exhausted who?

I am one exhausted unicorn. I need to lie down for a moment.

Knock, knock!

Who's there?

Mission.

Mission who?

I have a magical mission I have to do, but I will be back later.

Knock, knock!

Who's there?

Cracking.

Cracking who?

These jokes are cracking up my unicorn friends.

Knock, knock!

Who's there?

Meal.

Meal who?

That meal was amazing for us magical creatures.

Knock, knock!

Who's there?

Dog.

Dog who?

Did you know that dogs like unicorns too?

Knock, knock!

Who's there?

Where?

Where who?

Where did you go? We, unicorns, were so bored without you.

Knock, knock!

Who's there?

Clean up.

Clean up who?

You've got to clean up your room. Unicorns love clean spaces.

Knock, knock!

Who's there?

Shampoo.

Shampoo who?

You remember that it's time to shampoo your mane.

Knock, knock!

Who's there?

Cars.

Cars who?

Honey cars don't belong in unicorn school. Only unicorns do.

Knock, knock!
Who's there?
Carry.
Carry who?
I think some of the unicorns are getting carried away.

Knock, knock!
Who's there?
Been.
Been who?
The unicorns had to leave for a while. It's been a long time since we've seen you.

Knock, knock!
Who's there?
Hide.
Hide who?
Hide the unicorn's magic treasure where no one can find it.

Knock, knock!
Who's there?
Cloud.
Cloud who?
Every cloud has a silver lining.

Knock, knock!

Who's there?

Every.

Every who?

Every time we, unicorns, come over, we go through this.

Knock, knock!

Who's there?

Bathroom.

Bathroom who?

I need to go to the bathroom. Do you have one for unicorns?

Knock, knock!

Who's there?

Bowling.

Bowling who?

I don't know if unicorns bowl, but we'd love it if you came with us.

Knock, knock!

Who's there?

Eye.

Eye who.

Unicorns say an eye for an eye and a tooth for a tooth.

Knock, knock!

Who's there?

Are we.

Are we who?

Are we on the same page with this unicorn knock-knock jokes?

Knock, knock!

Who's there?

Apple.

Apple who?

An apple a day keeps the unicorn doctor away.

Knock, knock!

Who's there?

Drawing.

Drawing who?

It's back to the drawing board for me.

But sweetie, unicorns can't draw.

Knock, knock!

Who's there?

Sparkles.

Sparkles who?

Sparkles got glitter all over the wall.

Knock, knock!

Who's there?

Demand.

Demand who?

This unicorn demands a hug and kiss from you.

Knock, knock!

Who's there?

Music.

Music who?

I think all of us unicorns would like to listen to music today.

Knock, knock!

Who's there?

Cold.

Cold who?

Unicorns are not overly fond of extreme temperatures.

Knock, knock!

Who's there?

Drag.

Drag who?

If we want to have time to play, all of the unicorns need to stop dragging their feet and get to work.

Knock, knock!

Who's there?

Purse.

Purse who?

Don't you know that unicorns control the purse strings?

Knock, knock!

Who's there?

Lend.

Lend who?

I will lend you some money if you promise to pay me back this time.

Knock, knock!

Who's there?

Package.

Package who?

There's a magical package for the unicorns today.

Knock, knock!

Who's there?

Remember.

Remember who?

You know I don't remember which unicorn I was talking to.

Knock, knock!

Who's there?

Key.

Key who?

You've given the unicorns the wrong key. We can't play now.

Knock, knock!

Who's there?

Boo.

Boo who?

I'm sorry my unicorn jokes are so bad. I didn't mean to make you upset and cry.

Knock, knock!

Who's there?

Water.

Water who?

Are you unicorns still thirsty? There's plenty of water to go around.

Knock, knock!

Who's there?

Can you.

Can you who?

Can you open the door? You wouldn't make unicorns sleep outside, would you?

Knock, knock!

Who's there?

Glittery.

Glittery who?

How many other unicorns named glittery do you know?

Knock, knock!

Who's there?

Surrounded.

Surrounded who?

You're surrounded by unicorns. What are you going to do?

Knock, knock!

Who's there?

Beep.

Beep who.

Cars go beep, beep. Unicorns whinny.

Knock, knock!

Who's there?

Careful.

Careful who?

Be careful to keep your coats pretty and shiny.

Knock, knock!

Who's there?

Break.

Break who?

I think the unicorns are worn out from playing. I'm going to give them a break.

Knock, knock!

Who's there?

Shoe.

Shoe who?

We're not shoes being unicorns.

Knock, knock!

Who's there?

Peas.

Peas who?

We, unicorns, are peas in a pod.

Knock, knock!

Who's there?

Wish.

Wish who?

We have special unicorn wishes for you.

Knock, knock!

Who's there?

I wish.

I wish who?

I wish you a happy unicorn day.

Knock, knock!

Who's there?

Spaghetti and meatballs.

Spaghetti and meatballs who?

Spaghetti and meatballs are the best for unicorns!

Knock, knock!

Who's there?

Clean.

Clean who?

Don't forget to clean your hooves and tail today.

Knock, knock!

Who's there?

Christmas.

Christmas who?

The unicorns got to help Santa at Christmas!

Knock, knock!

Who's there?

Easter.

Easter who?

Do you know when the Easter bunny is coming?

He's a friend of ours.

Knock, knock!

Who's there?

Would you like.

Would you like who?

Would you like a chocolate bunny? All the unicorns do.

Knock, knock!

Who's there?

Fairies.

Fairies who?

Have you seen the fairies lately? We, unicorns, like to play with them, too.

Knock, knock!

Who's there?

Today.

Today who?

We unicorns say that today is the first day of the rest of your life.

Knock, knock!

Who's there?

Thank you.

Thank you who?

Thank you for inviting us unicorns into your lovely home.

Knock, knock!

Who's there?

Whinny.

Whinny who?

I'm sorry, are you speaking unicorn or owl?

Knock, knock!

Who's there?

Lost.

Lost who?

It looks like sparkly got lost on her way to see you.

Knock, knock!

Who's there?

Hoof.

Hoof who?

I think I have something stuck inside my hoof.

Knock, knock!

Who's there?

Unicorn.

Unicorn who?

Unicorns say don't count your cupcakes before they get baked.

Knock, knock!

Who's there?

Hot.

Hot who?

We, unicorns, should get some hot cocoa.

Knock, knock!

Who's there?

Far.

Far who?

So far, everything for us unicorns is good.

Knock, knock!

Who's there?

Hello.

Hello who?

Hello kitty. Did you know that unicorns love cats too?

Knock, knock!

Who's there?

Quack.

Quack who?

We've explained that unicorns don't make funny noises.

Knock, knock!
Who's there?
Pain.
Pain who?
It's pretty painful for a unicorn to have to keep knocking on the door. We have to use our snout.

Knock, knock!
Who's there?
Song.
Song who?
Have you ever heard the unicorn's song?

Knock, knock!
Who's there?
Medal.
Medal who?
Did you know that unicorns could medal in running?

Knock, knock!
Who's there?
Apple.
Apple who?

If you want to give a unicorn a healthy treat, give them an apple.

Knock, knock!

Who's there?

Happy.

Happy who?

Happy your unicorn friend came to see you today?

Knock, knock!

Who's there?

Cool.

Cool who?

The weather's nice and cool today. We can fly even higher.

Knock, knock!

Who's there?

Magic.

Magic who?

You're still a baby unicorn. You know mom said no magic without her.

Knock, knock!

Who's there?

Cereal.

Cereal who?

Unicorns like marshmallow cereal.

Knock, knock!

Who's there?

Dancing.

Dancing who?

Unicorns love dancing too!

Knock, knock!

Who's there?

Friends.

Friends who?

Unicorns are friends to all.

Knock, knock!

Who's there?

Movie.

Movie who?

Let's all go to the movies. Unicorns have special seating.

Knock, knock!

Who's there?

Color.

Color who?

Unicorns come in all shapes and colors.

Knock, knock!

Who's there?

Fine.

Fine who?

All of us unicorns are doing fine today. How are you?

Knock, knock!

Who's there?

Plane.

Plane who?

Unicorns don't need planes. We can fly.

Knock, knock!

Who's there?

Drums.

Drums who?

Do you have any idea how hard it is to play the drums with your hooves?

Knock, knock!

Who's there?

Eat.

Eat who?

Unicorns need to eat often. We get really hungry.

Knock, knock!
Who's there?
Glasses.
Glasses who?
Unicorns don't need glasses. They have great eyes.

Knock, knock!
Who's there?
Peppermint.
Peppermint who?
If unicorns like candy, do they like peppermint too?

Knock, knock!
Who's there?
Secret.
Secret who?
If I tell you a unicorn secret, you won't tell right?

Knock, knock!
Who's there?
Mommy.
Mommy who?
Mommy unicorn has come to see you.

Knock, knock!
Who's there?
Jolly.
Jolly who?
You're such a jolly unicorn!

Knock, knock!
Who's there?
Holly.
Holly who?
Did you know that Glittery is one holly jolly unicorn around Santa Claus?

Knock, knock!
Who's there?
Beware.
Beware.
Beware this Halloween, unicorns like to be mischievous.

Knock, knock!
Who's there?
Daddy.
Daddy who?
Daddy unicorn is here to play games with you.

Knock, knock!
Who's there?
Tissue.
Tissue who?
We have magical tissues that help when you're sneezing.

Knock, knock!
Who's there?
Scream.
Scream who?
The unicorns want to scream when we don't get to see you.

Knock, knock!
Who's there?
Know.
Know who?
You know us unicorns the best.

Knock, knock!
Who's there?
Uh, oh.
Uh, oh who?
Uh, oh, I think us unicorns have been here before.

Knock, knock!
Who's there?
I drew.
I drew who?
We used our magic to draw you.

Knock, knock!
Who's there?
Bee.
Bee who?
A bee just stung me. Be careful to make sure he doesn't do it to you too.

Knock, knock!
Who's there?
Bet.
Bet who?
I bet you couldn't tell that it was this unicorn at your door.

Knock, knock!
Who's there?
Me.
Me who?
You forgot which unicorn I am again?

Knock, knock!
Who's there?
Three.
Three who?
Three little unicorns playing in your kitchen.

Knock, knock!
Who's there?
Glad.
Glad who?
Aren't you glad the weekend is here? Now you and the unicorns can play all day.

Knock, knock!
Who's there?
Great.
Great who?
The unicorns had a great day playing magical games with you.

Knock, knock!
Who's there?
Wonderful.
Wonderful who?
Our friend, Pinky the unicorn, had a great time with you.

Knock, knock!

Who's there?

Hippo.

Hippo who?

Hippopotamuses love hanging out with unicorns.

Knock, knock!

Who's there?

Why.

Why who?

Why is it always me that's having to try and knock on the door? I'm a unicorn. I don't even have fingers.

Knock, knock!

Who's there?

Run.

Run who?

If you run with us, our magic will lift you higher!

Knock, knock!

Who's there?

Sore.

Sore who?

My snout is sore from trying to knock so much.

Knock, knock!
Who's there?
Bell.
Bell who?
Is your bell working? Two unicorns tried to ring it and we can't hear it at all?

Knock, knock!
Who's there?
How many.
How many who?
How many unicorns does it take to screw in a light bulb?
None, silly. Unicorns don't have fingers.

Knock, knock!
Who's there?
Cry.
Cry who?
The unicorns are crying because you won't them in to play with you.

Knock, knock!
Who's there?
Dinner.
Dinner who?
It's time for dinner, and the unicorns will get their cupcakes.

Knock, knock!

Who's there?

Excuse me.

Excuse me who?

Excuse me, would you mind scooting over? You are sitting on my tail

---

Knock, knock!

Who's there?

Kangaroo.

Kangaroo who?

The kangaroos are coming to join the unicorns on their picnic today.

Knock, knock!

Who's there?

Surprise.

Surprise who?

Glittery unicorn, pink, and blue all came to see you.

Knock, knock!

Who's there?

Party.

Party who?

The unicorns are having a tea and cake party, would you like to come too?

Knock, knock!

Who's there?

Awesome.

Awesome who?

Awesome day for unicorn knock-knock jokes, right?

Knock, knock!

Who's there?

Ignore.

Ignore who?

You ignored the unicorns at your door.

Knock, knock!

Who's there?

Mind.

Mind who?

Will you be able to make up your mind on whether or not you're going to let us unicorns come in or not?

Knock, knock!

Who's there?

Eat.

Eat who?

Do you know any good places for unicorns to eat?

Knock, knock!

Who's there?

Nice.

Nice who?

We, unicorns, had a really nice time with you today.

Knock, knock!

Who's there?

Grandpa.

Grandpa who?

It's your grandpa unicorn. Open the door and I have stories to tell you.

Knock, knock!

Who's there?

Grandma.

Grandma who?

Did you honestly think grandpa unicorn would come without grandma?

Knock, knock!

Who's there?

Bell.

Bell who?

Your bell is broken again. We will have to learn a new way to knock.

Knock, knock!

Who's there?

Run.

Run who?

Don't worry, sweetie. I won't run out of unicorn knock-knock jokes to tell you.

Knock, knock!

Who's there?

Sick.

Sick who?

So, are you sick of these unicorn knock-knock jokes? I hope not. We've got hundreds more.

Knock, knock!

Who's there?

Cops.

Cops who?

Have you ever played cops and robbers with a unicorn?

Knock, knock!

Who's there?

Silly.

Silly who?

Unicorns like to laugh, ask more silly questions.

Knock, knock!

Who's there?

Cookie.

Cookie who?

I have a special unicorn cookie, and I want to share it with you.

Knock, knock!

Who's there?

Sad.

Sad who?

The unicorns are sad that the door won't open.

Knock, knock!

Who's there?

See.

See who?

I will have to see you later. I am babysitting other unicorns today.

Knock, knock!

Who's there?

Water.

Water who?

Do you have any water? Unicorns get very thirsty.

Knock, knock!

Who's there?

Police.

Police who?

The unicorns are playing police officer!

Knock, knock!

Who's there?

Pass by.

Pass by who?

Glittery and the blue unicorn decided to pass by and see you today.

Knock, knock!

Who's there?

Pass.

Pass who?

Can you please pass the chicken? The unicorns got hungry again.

Knock, knock!

Who's there?

Mother.

Mother who?

The unicorns love playing mother, do you?

Knock, knock!

Who's there?

Pants.

Pants who?

Unicorns don't wear pants or shoes.

Knock, knock!

Quiet.

Quiet who?

You and the unicorns have to be quiet it's a library silly.

Knock, knock!

Who's there?

Quack, quack.

Quack, quack who?

The ducks would like to play with the unicorns today!

Knock, knock!

Who's there?

Leaving.

Leaving who?

If you tell another bad unicorn knock-knock joke, I am leaving.

Knock, knock!

Who's there?

Dance.

Dance who?

We, unicorns, are going to dance around the room.

Knock, knock!

Who's there?

Bark.

Bark who?

Your dog is barking. We unicorns can hear him. Why can't you?

Knock, knock!

Who's there?

Time.

Time who?

All the unicorns are on time to see you and your friends today.

Knock, knock!

Who's there?

Oops.

Oops who?

Oops, the unicorns have come to the wrong house again.

Knock, knock!

Who's there?

Questions.

Questions who?

Unicorns ask a lot of questions, don't they?

Knock, knock!

Who's there?

Stop.

Stop who?

Please stop tugging on my tail.

Knock, knock!

Who's there?

Green.

Green who?

Oh no, the purple unicorn is turning green. Are you feeling sick?

Knock, knock!

Who's there?

Thank you.

Thank you who?

The unicorns say, thank you for being awesomely you!

Knock, knock!

Who's there?

Five.

Five who?

Five unicorns and five unicorns make ten unicorns!

Knock, knock!

Who's there?

All.

All who?

Did you know that all of us animals are best friends with all the unicorns?

Knock, knock!

Who's there?

There.

There who?

If you need us the unicorns will be there for you.

Knock, knock!

Who's there?

Do you know.

Do you know who?

Do you know when auntie unicorn is coming home?

Knock, knock!

Who's there?

See.

See who?

The unicorns have good eyes. You can't hide from us, we can see you.

Knock, knock!

Who's there?

Monster.

Monster who?

Don't be afraid, the unicorns will protect you.

Knock, knock!

Who's there?

Why.

Why who?

Glittery unicorn doesn't know. Why are you asking me?

Knock, knock!

Who's there?

Eggs.

Eggs who?

Let's have eggs today. Unicorns love a healthy breakfast.

Knock, knock!

Who's there?

My house.

My house who?

We get to go to my house with rainbow unicorn today.

Knock, knock!

Who's there?

Follow.

Follow who?

You lead the way and the unicorns will follow you.

Knock, knock!

Who's there?

Cute.

Cute who?

Don't you think unicorns are super cute?

Knock, knock!

Who's there?

Little.

Little who?

I don't know. I'm just a little unicorn.

Knock, knock!

Who's there?

Carry.

Carry who?

If you need us to, the unicorns will carry you.

Knock, knock!

Who's there?

Magic.

Magic who?

The little unicorns need a magic nap before they play anymore.

Knock, knock!

Who's there?

Night.

Night who?

The unicorns must bid you goodnight. It's past their bedtime, and they have to sleep.

Knock, knock!

Who's there?

Be good.

Be good who?

Be good or mommy unicorn is going to fly you to the time-out chair.

Knock, knock!

Who's there?

Big.

Big who?

I am a big unicorn now!

Knock, knock!

Who's there?

Pants.

Pants who?

Our pants won't fit a unicorn.

Knock, knock!

Who's there?

Shoes.

Shoes who?

Unicorns don't wear shoes. They don't fit over our hooves.

Knock, knock!

Who's there?

Tie.

Tie who?

Unicorns can't tie shoes. You'll have to ask someone else to help you.

Knock, knock!

Who's there?

Walk.

Walk who?

This unicorn would walk a hundred miles to play games with you.

Knock, knock!
Who's there?
Al.
Al who?
Don't worry, the unicorns and alligators get along too.

Knock, knock!
Who's there?
Starving.
Starving who?
Do you have anything to eat? Unicorns need a lot of food, and they are starving again.

Knock, knock!
Who's there?
Go.
Go who?
If you go to the door, you'll see seven unicorns that are here to visit you.

Knock, knock!
Who's there?
Bugging.
Bugging who?

Are these unicorn knock-knock jokes bugging you?

Knock, knock!

Who's there?

Thump, thump.

Thump, thump who?

Thump, thump, thump, the bunny rabbits came to see the unicorns.

Knock, knock!

Who's there?

Bee.

Bee who?

Watch out, glittery unicorn, there is a bee on you.

Knock, knock!

Who's there?

Hug.

Hug who?

Funny you should ask. Have you hugged a unicorn yet?

Knock, knock!

Who's there?

Letter.

Letter who?

I sent a magical letter to you. Did you receive it yet?

Knock, knock!
Who's there?
Tail.
Tail who?
Why do you keep tugging on the poor unicorn's tail?

Knock, knock!
Who's there?
Stamp.
Stamp who?
The little unicorns are stamping because they are excited to see you.

Knock, knock!
Who's there?
Hide.
Hide who?
You have to find the littlest unicorn. She's hiding from you.

Knock, knock!
Who's there?
Two.
Two who?
Two unicorns can play that game.

Knock, knock!

Who's there?

Catch.

Catch who?

You'll have to catch up. The green unicorn is pretty far ahead of you.

Knock, knock!

Who's there?

Race.

Race who?

If you race the unicorns, do you think you can win?

Knock, knock!

Who's there?

Lying.

Lying who?

Are you lying to Sparkly unicorn? You need to tell the truth.

Knock, knock!

Who's there?

Lying.

Lying who?

We've been lying around all day. It's time to get up and have unicorn games.

Knock, knock!

Who's there?

Jump.

Jump who?

Did you know that unicorns can jump over the clouds?

Knock, knock!

Who's there?

When.

When who?

When can the unicorns stop all this knocking?

Knock, knock!

Who's there?

Milk.

Milk who?

Would you like some milk with your unicorn sugar cookies?

Knock, knock!

Who's there?

Tea.

Tea who?

Would you like to have tea and unicorn sandwiches with me?

Knock, knock!

Who's there?

Dark.

Dark who?

Don't be afraid of the dark. You've got the unicorns all around you.

Knock, knock!

Who's there?

Wrap.

Wrap who?

We need to wrap ourselves up. The unicorns all agree that it's too cold today.

Knock, knock!

Who's there?

Bees.

Bees who?

Bees keep stinging the unicorns. It must be a new season already.

Knock, knock!

Who's there?

Camping.

Camping who?

The unicorns are all going camping. Do you want to come?

Knock, knock!

Who's there?

Trees.

Trees who?

Unicorns love flying over the trees. They are so green!

Knock, knock!

Who's there?

Lunch.

Lunch who?

Mommy unicorn says it's time to come inside for lunch.

Knock, knock!

Who's there?

Fly.

Fly who?

Unicorns love to fly next to rainbows.

Knock, knock!

Who's there?

Tummy ache.

Tummy ache who?

The little unicorn ate too much and has a tummy ache.

Knock, knock!

Who's there?

Pie.

Pie who?

Unicorns love pie! Would you like a slice too?

Knock, knock!

Who's there?

Cookie.

Cookie who?

Are there any more unicorn cookies? They were so good.

Knock, knock!

Who's there?

Bawk, bawk, bawk.

Bawk, bawk, bawk who?

Bawk, bawk, bawk. The cute little chickens came to see the little unicorns.

Knock, knock!

Who's there?

Burnt.

Burnt who?

It looks like we burnt the unicorn's breakfast. I think we need to make it once more.

Knock, knock!

Who's there?

Horse.

Horse who?

The horses run quickly like the unicorns.

Knock, knock!

Who's there?

Unicorn.

Unicorn who?

Unicorn sense!

Knock, knock!

Who's there?

Delicious.

Delicious who?

Unicorns love eating delicious food.

Knock, knock!

Who's there?

Broccoli.

Broccoli who?

Bet you didn't know unicorns always finish their broccoli too.

Knock, knock!

Who's there?

Ham.

Ham who?

Can we feed the unicorns ham for breakfast today?

Knock, knock!

Who's there?

Whinny.

Whinny who?

The unicorn keeps whinnying. I think she wants your attention.

Knock, knock!

Who's there?

Chip.

Chip who?

Chocolate chip unicorn cookies.

Knock, knock!

Who's there?

Trouble.

Trouble who?

You'll be in trouble with grandma unicorn if you keep sassing her.

Knock, knock!

Who's there?

Pick,

Pick who?

Those big unicorns need to stop picking on the little ones.

Knock, knock!

Who's there?

Up.

Up who?

Let's turn up the music so the unicorns can hear it too.

Knock, knock!

Who's there?

Love.

Love who?

The unicorns will always have love for you.

Knock, knock!

Who's there?

Heart.

Heart who?

The unicorn's heart belongs to you.

Knock, knock!

Who's there?

Music.

Music who?

Listen closely you can hear the unicorns making pretty music.

Knock, knock!

Who's there?

Hooves.

Hooves who?

You've slammed my hooves into your door again.

Knock, knock!

Who's there?

Pretty.

Pretty who?

The unicorns think your house is very pretty.

Knock, knock!

Who's there?

Lost.

Lost who?

If you're lost, the unicorns will show you the way.

Knock, knock!

Who's there?

Mosquito.

Mosquito who?

The mosquitos are trying to bite the unicorns again.

Knock, knock!

Who's there?

Vampire.

Vampire who?

Do you think the unicorns would try to be vampires this Halloween?

Knock, knock!

Who's there?

Sad.

Sad who?

It's sad that you never recognize your unicorn friends.

Knock, knock!

Who's there?

Coat.

Coat who?

Glittery unicorn's coat is getting sparkly glitter everywhere.

Knock, knock!

Who's there?

Pretending.

Pretending who?

Are you pretending that you don't know who the unicorns are?

Knock, knock!

Who's there?

Recognize.

Recognize who?

You don't recognize mommy unicorn?

Knock, knock!

Who's there?

Pizza.

Pizza who?

I think the unicorns ate all of the pizza today.

Knock, knock!

Who's there?

Poem.

Poem who?

The unicorns used their magic to write you a poem.

Knock, knock!

Who's there?

Rainbow.

Rainbow who?

Oh look! You can see the unicorns playing next to the rainbow.

Knock, knock!

Who's there?

Better.

Better who?

I better not tell you. It's a special unicorn secret.

Knock, knock!

Who's there?

Clear.

Clear who?

You'll have to clear the way. The unicorns can't fit through.

Knock, knock!

Who's there?

Ice cream.

Ice cream who?

The unicorns had ice cream today because it was so hot.

Knock, knock!

Who's there?

Valentine.

Valentine who?

Would you like to be the unicorn's valentine today?

Knock, knock!

Who's there?

Bless.

Bless who?

The unicorns didn't sneeze. Did you?

Knock, knock!

Who's there?

Presents.

Presents who?

Be careful with those presents. There for the unicorns and they are fragile.

Knock, knock!

Who's there?

Hand.

Hand who?

We'd like to hold your hand, but unicorns don't have fingers.

Knock, knock!

Who's there?

Crowd.

Crowd who?

Unicorns love hanging out in a crowd with all their friends.

Knock, knock!

Who's there?

Again.

Again who?

These unicorn knock-knock jokes are so funny we could hear them again and again.

Knock, knock!

Who's there?

Nice.

Nice who?

Unicorns are nice and sweet.

Knock, knock!

Who's there?

Vacation?

Vacation who?

Where would the unicorns go on vacation?

Knock, knock!

Who's there?

Early.

Early who?

Unicorns say, early to bed, early to rise, and then you will have a fantastic way to fly.

Knock, knock!

Who's there?

Grandpa.

Grandpa who?

Grandpa unicorn has some great stories for you.

Knock, knock!

Who's there?

Cake.

Cake who?

The unicorns have a cake for your birthday.

Knock, knock!

Who's there?

Super.

Super who?

Super unicorns have awesome special abilities.

Knock, knock!

Who's there?

Football.

Football who?

Can unicorns play football with us in the park?

Knock, knock!

Who's there?

Uncle.

Uncle who?

Your aunt and uncle unicorn came all the way to see you.

Knock, knock!

Who's there?

Santa.

Santa who?

The unicorns found Santa and he has presents for you.

Knock, knock!

Who's there?

Coal.

Coal who?

No one gives coals to the unicorns on Christmas.

Knock, knock!

Who's there?

Nickel.

Nickel who?

Grandpa unicorn says nickels used to be worth so much more.

Knock, knock!

Who's there?

Blood.

Blood who?

The unicorn vampires want to suck your blood!

Knock, knock!

Who's there?

Monster.

Monster who?

Oh, that's not a monster. That's a unicorn dressed in a costume.

Knock, knock!

Who's there?

Tie.

Tie who?

The unicorns tied for the race.

Knock, knock!

Who's there?

Forgot.

Forgot who?

I forgot which unicorn we are supposed to be looking for.

Knock, knock!

Who's there?

Can't.

Can't what?

You can't ask me, it's a unicorn secret and I'm not supposed to tell.

Knock, knock!
Who's there?
Stranger.
Stranger who?
Unicorns say never talk to strangers.

Knock, knock!
Who's there?
Remember.
Remember who?
You were supposed to remember to bring the unicorns to the game.

Knock, knock!
Who's there?
Sick.
Sick who?
Sparkly unicorn had to miss school because she was so sick.

Knock, knock!
Who's there?
Birthday.
Birthday who?
The unicorns wish you a happy birthday!

Knock, knock!

Who's there?

Adorable.

Adorable who?

Adorable unicorns are wishing you the best birthday ever.

Knock, knock!

Who's there?

Don't.

Don't who?

Don't open your presents yet. The unicorns said wait till Christmas.

Knock, knock!

Who's there?

Birthday.

Birthday who?

The unicorns made you a special magic cake for your birthday!

Knock, knock!

Who's there?

Fruit.

Fruit who?

Unicorns always finish their fruits and veggies to stay healthy.

Knock, knock!

Who's there?

Television.

Television who?

Do unicorns watch television like we do?

Knock, knock!

Who's there?

Forgotten.

Forgotten who?

The unicorns forgot who they were supposed to be talking to.

Knock, knock!

Who's there?

Help.

Help who?

I need the unicorns to help me with something.

Knock, knock!

Who's there?

Why.

Why who?

The unicorns want to know why you're always asking who?

Knock, knock!

Who's there?

Manners.

Manners who?

Unicorns say you should always mind your manners.

Knock, knock!

Who's there?

Unicorns.

Unicorns who?

It's snowing and the unicorns want to play with you.

Knock, knock!

Who's there?

Friends.

Friends who?

The unicorns will always be friends with you.

Knock, knock!

Who's there?

Door.

Door who?

You left the door shut, so the unicorns can't see anything including you.

Knock, knock!

Who's there?

Father?

Father who?

Like father unicorn, like son unicorn.

Knock, knock!

Who's there?

Silly.

Silly who?

You know the unicorns, silly. Let us in, so we don't get too cold, please.

Knock, knock!

Who's there?

Mane.

Mane who?

Sweetie, you have to comb your mane before going to unicorn school.

Knock, knock!

Who's there?

Guess.

Guess who?

Guess which unicorn is at your door today?

Knock, knock!

Who's there?

Go.

Go who?

The unicorns will go anywhere that you want them to.

Knock, knock!

Who's there?

Hula.

Hula who?

I would love to see a unicorn trying to hula hoop.

Knock, knock!

Who's there?

Cocoa.

Cocoa who?

The unicorns have cocoa and marshmallows tonight.

Knock, knock!

Who's there?

Bees.

Bees who?

The bees are buzzing so loud it is hurting the unicorn's ears.

Knock, knock!

Who's there?

Unicorn.

Unicorn who?

The unicorns are racing in the fields and spreading joy.

Knock, knock!

Who's there?

Unicorn.

Unicorn who?

The unicorns are watching the little ones today.

Knock, knock!

Who's there?

Be.

Be who?

The unicorns say we should always be ourselves.

Knock, knock!

Who's there?

How many?

How many who?

How many unicorns can fit in one room?

As many as they want, they are magic.

Knock, knock!

Who's there?

School.

School who?

A unicorn's favorite subject is flying!

Knock, knock!

Who's there?

Pressing.

Pressing who?

The unicorns would stay but they have very pressing matters to attend to.

Knock, knock!

Who's there?

Fish.

Fish who?

The unicorns saved the fish from the hot day and were able to have fun!

Knock, knock!

Who's there?

Happy.

Happy who?

I am so happy that my friends are unicorns.

Knock, knock!
Who's there?
Mane.
Mane who?
I hate when my mane gets tangled. It takes mommy unicorn forever to unravel.

Knock, knock!
Who's there?
Family.
Family who?
Unicorns love their family more than anything in the world.

Knock, knock!
Who's there?
Left.
Left who?
The unicorns were sad when they left. They were having fun with you.

Knock, knock!
Who's there?
Remember?
Remember who?

Remember me? I am your best friend. You can't forget your unicorn friends.

Knock, knock!

Who's there?

Karate.

Karate who?

The unicorns know how to karate with magic.

Knock, knock!

Who's there?

Find.

Find who?

We were playing hide and seek with the little unicorns and can't seem to find out where they were hidden.

Knock, knock!

Who's there?

Found.

Found who?

We looked and looked all around and after a while, the little unicorns were found.

Knock, knock!

Who's there?

Ho, ho.

Ho, ho who?

Unicorns say, when imitating Santa, you must say ho, ho, ho.

Knock, knock!

Who's there?

Love.

Love who?

Do you love blue unicorn? Because he loves you!

Knock, knock!

Who's there?

Cashew.

Cashew who?

Do you like cashews? The unicorns love walnuts.

Knock, knock!

Who's there?

Live.

Live who?

You have new neighbors. Unicorns moved in next door to you.

Knock, knock!

Who's there?

Summer

Summer who?

Unicorns love to fly in the clouds during summer.

Knock, knock!

Who's there?

Birds.

Birds who?

Birds fly high, but unicorns fly higher.

Knock, knock!

Who's there?

Have to go.

Have to go who?

I'm sorry, but the unicorns have to go home so they can finish their homework.

Knock, knock!

Who's there?

Remember.

Remember who?

Remember that when you eat, be like the unicorns, and chew your food thoroughly before you swallow.

Knock, knock!

Who's there?

Halloween.

Halloween who?

This Halloween, let's make sure the unicorns don't eat all of the candy from trick or treating.

Knock, knock!

Who's there?

Treats.

Treats who?

The unicorns always know where to get good treats!

Knock, knock!

Who's there?

Presents.

Presents who?

If you open the door, you will see the presents that the unicorns made for you.

Knock, knock!

Who's there?

Prancing.

Prancing who?

Do you think that you can prance like the unicorns do when they are happy?

Knock, knock!
Who's there?
Swimming.
Swimming who?
It's very hot today. We should all go swimming and take the little unicorns.

Knock, knock!
Who's there?
Partridge.
Partridge who?
The unicorns want to see the partridge in the pear tree.

Knock, knock!
Who's there?
Tag.
Tag who?
The unicorns are playing tag and now pink unicorn gets to be it!

Knock, knock!
Who's there?
Walk.
Walk who?
The unicorns all went on a sunny walk in the park today.

Knock, knock!

Who's there?

Terrific.

Terrific who?

The unicorns want you to have a terrific and magical day!

Knock, knock!

Who's there?

Moo.

Moo who?

Cows say moo, not unicorns.

Knock, knock!

Who's there?

Gobble, gobble.

Gobble, gobble who?

The unicorns love seeing the turkeys when they gobble, gobble!

Knock, knock!

Who's there?

Scream.

Scream who?

The unicorns won't scream but they really would like to spend time with you.

Knock, knock!

Who's there?

Pegasus.

Pegasus who?

Unicorns and Pegasus's are the very best of friends.

Knock, knock!

Who's there?

Family.

Family who?

A unicorn will always be able to depend on their family.

Knock, knock!

Who's there?

Pancakes.

Pancakes who?

Did you know that pancakes are a fun breakfast that unicorns love to eat?

Knock, knock!

Who's there?

Tune.

Tune who?

Unicorns can't tune instruments.

Knock, knock!

Who's there?

Running.

Running who?

It's funny how the unicorns keep running into you here.

Knock, knock!

Who's there?

Parents.

Parents who?

Unicorn parents need to round up the little ones.

Knock, knock!

Who's there?

Eggs.

Eggs who?

We're having eggs for breakfast. Did you want to join us and the unicorns to eat the eggs, too?

Knock, knock!

Who's there?

Tired.

Tired who?

Unicorns get tired of people lying to them.

Knock, knock!

Who's there?

One.

One who?

Unicorns are big there's only room for one of us to lay down here.

Knock, knock!

Who's there?

Chilly.

Chilly who?

The unicorns are getting really chilly waiting outside.

Knock, knock!

Who's there?

Deny.

Deny who?

Deny me the pleasure of another unicorn knock-knock joke please.

Knock, knock!

Who's there?

Up.

Up who?

If you're up, can you please let the unicorns in from outside?

Knock, knock!

Who's there?

Let's go.

Let's go who?

Let's all go to the beach and watch the sunset with the unicorns.

Knock, knock!

Who's there?

Had to.

Had to who?

Had to see you and the unicorns having so much fun!

Knock, knock!

Who's there?

Ran.

Ran who?

We ran all the way over here to tell the unicorns about a party!

Knock, knock!

Who's there?

Man.

Man who?

Man, we're sick of hearing all these unicorn knock-knock jokes.

Aren't you?

Knock, knock!
Who's there?
Never.
Never who?
I bet you've never had such awesome friends like our herd of unicorns.

Knock, knock!
Who's there?
Last.
Last who?
This would be the last unicorn knock-knock joke.

Knock, knock!
Who's there?
Just kidding.
Just kidding who?
This is actually the last knock-knock joke!

Conclusion

Thanks for making it through to the end of *Karen's Unicorn Knock Knock Jokes: The Magical Door That Spurts Rainbow Endlessly*. Let's hope it was entertaining and able to provide you with a few hours of excitement as you worked through the jokes.

Remember to claim your free book (Link at the front of the book) and also check out our other books that can be found on our Facebook page www.facebook.com/bluesourceandfriends.

Finally, if you found this book useful in any way, a review on Amazon is always appreciated!

Karen J. Bun